Hawaii's Past in a World of Pacific Islands

James M. Bayman
Thomas S. Dye

With maps by Eric K. Komori

SOCIETY FOR AMERICAN ARCHAEOLOGY

The SAA Press

The Society for American Archaeology, Washington, D.C. 20005
Copyright © 2013 by the Society for American Archaeology
All rights reserved. Published 2013

Printed in the United States of America

Library of Congress Cataloging-in-Publication Data

Bayman, James.
 Hawaii's past in a world of Pacific Islands / James M. Bayman, Thomas S. Dye with maps by
Eric K. Komori.
    pages cm
 ISBN 978-0-932839-54-1 (alk. paper)
 1. Hawaii--Civilization. 2. Hawaii--Antiquities. 3. Hawaii--History. 4. Ethnology--Hawaii.
 5. Hawaiians--Social life and customs. I. Title.
 DU624.5.B38 2013
 996.9'02--dc23
                              2013001183

Printed on acid-free paper

Contents

Acknowledgments

W e offer our thanks to Ken Ames (SAA Press Editor) and Paul Minnis (former SAA Press Editor) for their encouragement as we developed this book; it was our pleasure to engage in this writing project with their support. Guidance with the production of the manuscript was kindly provided by John Neikirk, Publications Manager for the Society for American Archaeology (SAA).

We are particularly grateful for our friends and colleagues in Hawai'i and elsewhere who have, for many years, shared their perspectives on the archaeology and history of the archipelago. We owe a special debt to Pat Kirch, John Peterson, and one anonymous reviewer for their careful and useful comments on the first draft of this book. The time and effort that they devoted to providing us their input is much appreciated. Rob Hommon, Dave Tuggle, Tim Rieth, Thegn Ladefoged, and Mark McCoy contributed greatly to the lines of thought developed in Chapters 3 and 4, without necessarily agreeing with all or any of it. Many of the ideas in Chapter 8 were initially developed with Maria Ka'imi Orr and Lynette Cruz. We thank them for stimulating discussions and hope that they see their influence on what we have written. Errors of fact or interpretation are ours alone.

We appreciate the editorial assistance of Krickette Murabayashi, research assistant at T. S. Dye & Colleagues, Archaeologists, for editing the book with her usual fine attention to detail and converting the LaTeX document to Word for submittal to The SAA Press.

Infrastructural support for writing this book was provided by the Anthropology Department of the University of Hawai'i–Mānoa and by T. S. Dye & Colleagues, Archaeologists.

We thank the following colleagues and institutions for permission to reproduce figures and photographs: Thegn Ladefoged for Figure 4.4; Yosihiko

Sinoto for Figure 5.5; Bishop Museum Press for Figure 6.1; and Bishop Museum for Figures 5.1, 7.1, and 7.2.

The authors have donated their royalties from sales of the book to the SAA scholarship program for Native Americans, Alaska Natives, Native Hawaiians, and Indigeneous Pacific Islanders.

1

Approaches to Hawaii's Past

Hawaii's first archaeologist, John F. G. Stokes, arrived in the islands from Australia in 1899, a year after Hawai'i was annexed by the United States of America and six years after the illegal overthrow of the Kingdom of Hawai'i in 1893 by a small band of insurgents supported by the American minister and United States troops (Sai 2011). This was an era when the decline and extinction of the Hawaiian "race" was widely predicted. From the start, the work of the archaeologists took place in abandoned cultural landscapes, places where traditional houses and temples had been reduced to their foundations, and the verdant agricultural fields described with admiration by Captain Cook and his crew a century earlier were overgrown with weeds. Since that time, archaeologists have joined the effort to construct a narrative of Hawaii's history along Western lines, a project that, unwittingly or not, has often served the interests of a newly dominant social and political order. This work of rewriting history has been taken up not just by archaeologists, but by a broad range of both native and Western scholars drawn from the ranks of historians, folklorists, politicians, clergy, and businessmen. It has considered several sources of evidence ranging widely over oral tradition, comparative linguistics and ethnology, memory culture, and the material remains that are properly the study of archaeology. This book chronicles archaeology's role in rewriting Hawaii's history. Its concern is the archaeological record of old Hawai'i—the material remnants of labor carried out from the time the islands were discovered by Polynesians late in the first millennium A.D. through the early decades of settlement by Americans and Europeans in the nineteenth century—and how this record has been used, and in some cases misused, to rewrite Hawaiian history. The book is not an argument for privileging archaeological data or interpretations, both of which we regard as important but inherently problematic.

Rather, it traces how archaeology and its concepts have developed in the unique cultural and social milieu of twentieth- and early twenty-first-century Hawai'i.

Perspectives on Ancient Hawai'i

Humanity's adventure in the most remote archipelago on earth began when the first canoe of Polynesians stepped on Hawaii's shores about a millennium ago. To sustain themselves, the Polynesians brought a suite of resources from the South Pacific, including chickens, dogs, and pigs, and various tropical plants such as taro, banana, coconut, and sugarcane. As the first people to settle the islands, Hawaii's earliest Polynesians were free to experiment with constructing a new society, unhindered by a pre-existing human population. Such opportunities were exceedingly rare in the Late Holocene world, except in the pristine islands that dotted the Pacific Ocean, a vast body of water covering some two-thirds of the globe. The Hawaiian Islands were among the last places on earth to witness human colonization and eventual contact with the West (Figure 1.1).

From an Americanist perspective, the timing of this event is remarkable. Hawaii's first recorded contact with Europeans ensued almost three centuries after natives in the Americas encountered agents of the Spanish Empire, and only two years after the Declaration of Independence of the United States of America was signed in 1776 C.E. in Philadelphia, Pennsylvania. Moreover, unlike Hawai'i, many native societies in North America experienced the consequences of Western contact several decades prior to any face-to-face encounter. Some native communities in North America, for example, experienced the ravages of introduced diseases and precipitous declines in their population decades prior to the arrival of Europeans in their immediate territories. Consequently, documentary accounts of those encounters describe the remnants of demographically and politically diminished societies (Upham 1982).

The Hawaiian Islands, in contrast, offer archaeology an exceptional opportunity to study the development of a society that was recorded in both native oral traditions and written documents before it was changed by non-Polynesian cultures and world capitalism. Since the moment of Hawaii's discovery, people from all walks of life have spun a tapestry of interpretations of its past. Today's Hawaiians recall traditions about their ancestral genealogies;

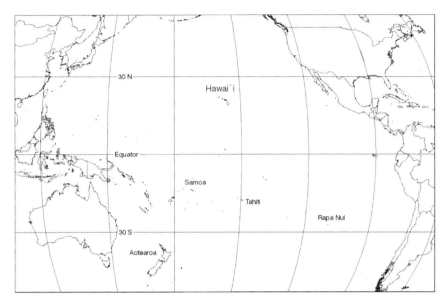

Figure 1.1: Location of Hawai'i in the Pacific Ocean.

these origin stories are transmitted across successive generations, from elders to their children. These traditions embody a legacy of gods, earthly creation, and human agency that enlivens the Hawaiian present with the past.

When Hawai'i encountered the West in 1778 C.E., the famed British naval captain James Cook and his crew penned the earliest accounts of her people's lifeways. At the time, Cook and his crew were sailing north to the Arctic Sea on the ships *Discovery* and *Resolution* in their search for a northwest passage from England to the Pacific Ocean. Their descriptions of Hawai'i and its people captivated the imagination of Western thinkers and artists who pondered the origin and meaning of Hawai'i and her people's membership in James Cook's idea of a Polynesian "Nation" (Beaglehole 1967:354). More than two centuries later, people around the world maintain a fascination with the magnificence of Hawaii's islands and her storied past.

Hawaiian oral traditions offer a uniquely native view of Hawaii's cultural past (Hommon 1976; Kirch 2010a). These traditions celebrate and commemorate Hawaii's primal creation, the feats of a pantheon of deities, and the genealogies of chiefly luminaries. Such traditions were recorded by indigenous Hawaiians who were schooled and influenced by Protestant Christian missionaries who first came to the islands in 1821. Native writers

3

in the mid-nineteenth century such as David Malo (1951), Samuel Kamakau (1961, 1964, 1976), John Papa ʻĪʻī (1963), and Kepelino (Beckwith 2007) set down traditions that had been passed on to them along with their own firsthand accounts of life in old Hawaiʻi. Other accounts were gathered and synthesized critically by Abraham Fornander (Fornander 1916–1919, 1969), who quizzed elderly Hawaiians about their daily lives with a particular focus on customs that prevailed before contact with Europeans. Because Hawaiian culture, traditions, and technologies changed rapidly in the decades following Cook's early visits, much of what these writers documented comprised "memory culture." Archaeologists who use the direct historic approach to interpret Hawaii's past view such writings as canonical sources (Nogelmeier 2010); such sources have long been a mainstay of studies of the precontact horizon in the islands. Structuralist analyses of these materials have yielded deep insights into traditional Hawaiian politics and religion (Valeri 1985a, 1985b, 1990, 1991).

The promise of archaeology in Hawaiʻi was initially constrained by an assumption that was widely shared by scholars: human occupation of the Pacific islands was relatively recent and so study of their peoples should be the purview of ethnographers. The relative shallowness of archaeological deposits in Hawaiʻi and elsewhere in the Pacific, compared to other regions of the world, seemingly corroborated this belief. If Hawaii's past was relatively brief, it was implied, ethnographic studies of its native peoples were more vital than archaeological studies for documenting traditional lifeways and technologies. Early ethnographic studies benefited from the rich collections held by Bishop Museum, established in 1890 as a treasure house of the Kamehameha dynasty (Rose 1980), and later augmented by important, well-preserved collections of Hawaiian material culture (Summers 1999). Bishop Museum collections at the turn of the twentieth century included a rich array of material culture such as wood canoes, plant-fiber fishnets, gourd containers, wood and stone bowls, wood spears and shark-tooth knives, stone adzes, and stone *poi* pounders. Other materials included barkcloth; plaited mats; feather capes, cloaks, helmets; and ritual "standards," sacred images made of stone, wood, and feathers (Brigham 1899, 1902; Buck 1957; Rose et al. 1993).

Emergence of Archaeology

The first systematic records of Hawaiian archaeological field remains were made by an antiquarian and publisher, Thomas G. Thrum, who compiled descriptions of temples and their associated legends for publication in an almanac (Thrum 1906–1907a, 1906–1907b, 1915, 1916). Hawaii's first major archaeological field project was initiated in 1906 when Bishop Museum sent Stokes to map ancient temples on Hawai'i Island (Dye 1989:4–5; Stokes 1991). Stokes was charged with the task of producing plans of known temple foundations and compiling accounts of their history from elderly Hawaiians (Dye 1989:5–6). Although traditional gods were no longer openly worshipped at these temples following the overthrow of the traditional religion in 1819, it was thought that plans of heiau foundations could be integrated with Hawaiian genealogies to track the arrival of Pa'ao, a legendary priest from an island in the South Pacific. In traditional accounts, Pa'ao introduced a religious ideology that sustained a pantheon of gods, legitimized class stratification, and compelled offerings and human sacrifice at large war temples. After he returned from Hawai'i Island, Stokes completed the first "rescue archaeology" project in the islands, recording the walled fish traps of Pearl Harbor in advance of its eventual development as the world's largest naval base (Stokes 1909b). He also published notes on Hawaiian petroglyphs (Stokes 1909a).

A conscious attempt to build a more scientific archaeology at Bishop Museum developed in the 1920s and 1930s under the directorship of the Yale University geologist Herbert Gregory. Gregory brought graduate student archaeologists to Hawai'i to complete island surveys of a broad range of sites. In addition to the temples, fish traps, and petroglyphs recorded by Stokes, the graduate students identified and recorded a wide variety of feature types, including house sites and villages, shelter caves, fishing shrines, fishponds, battle sites, trails, *hōlua* slides, burial grounds, and agricultural terraces, among others (Bennett 1931; Emory 1924, 1928; McAllister 1933a, 1933b; Sterling 1998; Summers 1971). They looked for evidence of superposition of architectural elements with the goal of weaning archaeology from its dependence on tradition for chronology, but failed to find any examples.

It was not until the University of Hawai'i offered a field school course in 1950 that the potential time-depth of Hawaii's past was fully realized. The archaeological field training program was directed by Kenneth P. Emory, a Bishop Museum archaeologist, shortly before it was announced that ^{14}C dating had been developed by the University of Chicago physicist Willard F. Libby. The application of ^{14}C dating to a charcoal sample from the field school excavations at a rockshelter indicated that it was apparently occupied about a millennium ago. The recovery of datable charcoal from the lowest level of a stratified rockshelter electrified the archaeologists who wrote that "it opened up undreamed of possibilities for reconstructing the prehistory of the area" (Emory in Emory et al. 1968:ix).

Like other Americanist archaeologists, fieldworkers in the Hawaiian Islands quickly sought to construct a culture-historical chronology of the past. Unlike their colleagues who excavated in the eastern or southwestern United States, Hawaii's archaeologists did not recover ceramics or projectile points, two mainstays of culture-historical chronologies across the Americas. Instead, archaeologists in Hawai'i undertook detailed analyses of fishhooks from stratified deposits to construct time-sensitive sequences of technological change in the islands (e.g., Emory et al.1968; Sinoto 1968; Emory and Sinoto 1969).

Subsequent attempts to construct culture-historical chronologies focused on Hawaiian stone adzes within the larger geographic framework of East Polynesia (Duff 1959; Emory 1968). The prevailing theoretical perspective held that similarities in the forms of adzes from different island groups were due to historical connections among the people of the island groups, rather than to technological and functional constraints in the production and use of these stone woodworking tools. The typical quadrangular-sectioned, tanged Hawaiian adze has close parallels in Eastern Polynesia, but is distinct from the adzes typical of Western Polynesia, and this was interpreted as evidence for close culture-historical relationships in Eastern Polynesia. Although preliminary suggestions of chronological significance for adze form were offered (Kirch 1972, 1985), subsequent investigations indicated that their morphological variability is due to differences in function and use life rather than age (Cleghorn 1992). Archaeologists became increasingly reluctant to rely on variation in stone adze morphology to construct a culture-historical chronology for Hawaii's past, and have focused instead on technological explanations for the forms of Hawaiian stone adzes (Cleghorn 1982, 1984).

Growth of Archaeology

In certain respects, the 1960s and 1970s witnessed the heyday of Hawaii's archaeology and its contributions to the New Archaeology. The rise of cultural resource management in the wake of intensified economic development that followed statehood in 1959 sustained a new generation of archaeologists in the islands. Archaeology in Hawai'i was no longer the sole province of Bishop Museum and the University of Hawai'i, and it was increasingly practiced by private-sector institutions in contract with government agencies and land developers. Still, some of the most innovative research originated was undertaken by the Museum and the University. Researchers employed at the Museum and the University pioneered the application of hydration-rind dating of volcanic glass (Morgenstein and Riley 1974) and later demonstrated its serious limitations (Olson 1983). Because volcanic glass flakes are ubiquitous at many Hawaiian sites and hydration-rind dating was relatively inexpensive, the typological classification and/or seriation of artifacts such as fishhooks and adzes or architectural features such as temples to construct chronologies assumed less importance in archaeology. Interest in seriation, with an emphasis on architecture rather than portable artifacts, was revived only recently (Graves and Cachola-Abad 1996; McElroy 2004; McCoy et al. 2011; Mulrooney and Ladefoged 2005).

Instead, archaeologists in Hawai'i turned their attention to the analysis and interpretation of subsistence, settlement, and political organization (e.g., Cordy 1981; Earle 1977, 1978). Their study of these topics was instigated by the rising influence of neo-evolutionary theory in Americanist archaeology and a belief that the broad chronological outlines of culture-history had been sufficiently well established in many regions. In Hawai'i, waning interest in a conventional culture-historical chronology stemmed, in part, from an assumption that ^{14}C dating and hydration-rind dating of volcanic glass are sufficient techniques to document change, even if artifact-based studies of fishhooks and adzes were problematic.

With leadership by Roger C. Green, archaeologists at Bishop Museum and the University conducted settlement pattern studies on the island of O'ahu in Mākaha Valley (Green 1969, 1970, 1980), at Lapakahi on Hawai'i Island (Newman 1970; Rosendahl 1972, 1994; Tuggle and Griffin 1973), and at Hālawa Valley on Moloka'i Island (Kirch and Kelly 1975) (Figure 1.2). These projects broke from earlier practice, which focused on the larger

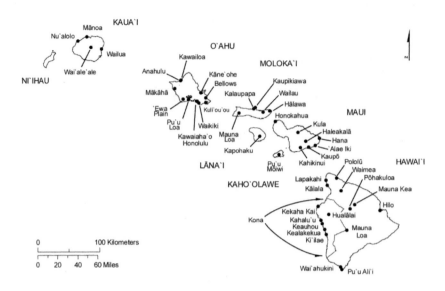

Figure 1.2: Place names mentioned in the text.

structures or those with the most excavation potential, and documented a full spectrum of features related to agricultural production, domestic habitation, and religious practices at temples. These path-breaking settlement pattern studies were followed by others across the archipelago (Cordy 1981; Earle 1978) and in the 1980s served as the model for inventory survey required by the State of Hawai'i under its historic preservation law. These and other studies (Cordy and Kaschko 1980; Kirch 1990; Weisler and Kirch 1985) applied the direct historic approach to interpret the subsistence and political economies of Hawaiian households, polities, and society before their contact with Europeans. Documenting and explaining the organization and development of chiefdoms (Earle 1978; Kirch 1984; Kolb 1994; Spriggs 1988; Tainter 1973) and early states (Allen 1991; Hommon 1976, 1986; Kolb 2006) through the detection of archaeological correlates of contact-period Hawaiian society was—and still is—a central goal of many scholars (Cordy 2000, 2004; Hommon 2010; Kirch 2010a; Kolb and Dixon 2002). Like their colleagues in the Americas and elsewhere who practice anthropological archaeology, archaeologists in Hawai'i have undertaken studies of monumentality, mortuary practices, and craft production and distribution to study the ancient political economy.

For example, studies of lithic resource extraction and circulation also intensified in Hawaiian archaeology in the 1980s, and this trend continues unabated. The application of artifact characterization techniques, such as petrography (Cleghorn et al. 1985; Lass 1994; Weisler 1990) and geochemical sourcing (Bayman and Moniz-Nakamura 2001; Collerson and Weisler 2007; Kirch et al. 2012; Lundblad et al. 2008; Mills et al. 2008; Mintmier 2007; Weisler 1998a), captured the attention of archaeologists. The analysis of stone quarries, volcanic glass debitage, and basalt adzes received particular attention in efforts to document the extraction, circulation, and discard of stone tools (Williams 2004). More recently, archaeologists have applied lithic characterization techniques to plant processing tools, such as *poi* pounders, and anthropomorphic images (Mills et al. 2010).

Contemporary Archaeology

The bulk of archaeology in Hawai'i is produced as Cultural Resource Management (CRM) reports. Unlike some regions of the Americas, such as southwestern and eastern North America, CRM operates in a sphere that rarely intersects the world of academic archaeology. Thus, it is not surprising that archaeology in Hawai'i has, for better or worse, largely escaped the critical scrutiny of post-processual approaches to the past (cf. Kawelu 2007; Spriggs 1989, 1991). With relatively few exceptions (e.g., Bayman 2008; Flexner 2010; Kirch 2004; Kirch and Sahlins 1992; Masse 1995; McCoy 1999), archaeologists in the Hawaiian Islands continue to emphasize the ecological and economic imperatives that influenced the nature of human and non-human interaction and/or the development of early complex societies (e.g., Cordy 2004; Dixon et al. 2002; Hommon 2010; Kirch 2010a; Kolb 2006). Studies of agricultural production are the foundation of most research on Hawaiian political economy (e.g., Earle 1978, 1980, 1997; Hommon 2010; Kirch 1994, 2010a; Kirch, ed. 2010; Mulrooney and Ladefoged 2005). Although some archaeologists have considered under-researched dimensions of gender relations (e.g., Kirch and O'Day 2003; Van Gilder 2001) in ancient Hawai'i, and other topics like archaeoastronomy (e.g., Chauvin 2000; Liller 2000; Meech and Warther 1996; Ruggles 1999, 2001; Kirch 2004), their efforts are departures from the norm.

The most recent incarnation of environmentally oriented archaeology in Hawai'i has been the National Science Foundation-funded "Hawai'i Biocomplexity Project" (Kirch, ed. 2010). Participants in this international research program include archaeologists and scientists from the University of California, Berkeley and Santa Clara, the University of New Mexico, the University of Auckland in New Zealand, and Stanford University, among others. This research project was centered on the study of "coupled socio-natural systems" in selected areas in the Hawaiian Islands. Documenting the varying potential of different landscapes for food production (e.g., Ladefoged et al. 2003; Ladefoged and Graves 2006; Ladefoged et al. 2009; Vitousek et al. 2004), and the organization of the human communities that were sustained by these systems, was a central dimension of the research agenda.

Contemporary research in the islands is benefiting from a suite of innovative techniques for sharply illuminating specific details of the Hawaiian past. The application of Bayesian statistics in chronometric dating (Dye 2010; Dye 2011a, 2011b; Dye and Pantaleo 2010) uses stratigraphic information to constrain the results of ^{14}C calibration. The precision achieved by the Bayesian method is especially useful with the short Hawaiian cultural sequence, which is measured in centuries rather than millennia. ^{230}Th dating of branch coral offers the ability to secure precise age determinations with standard deviations on the order of five years. Applications of the method to pieces of branch coral interpreted as offerings on ancient religious shrines and temples and to construction fill material (Kirch and Sharp 2005; Weisler et al. 2005) hold out the promise of chronometric precision for studies of architectural and ideological development, but also introduce novel problems of context and association (Dye 2010:146–147). Analysis of plant micro-fossils such as starch grains, phytoliths, xylem cells, and pollen has provided direct evidence of the actual crops, such as sweet potato and banana, that were cultivated in presumed agricultural features (Horrocks and Rechtman 2009; Pearsall and Trimble 1984). Finally, non-destructive geochemical characterization of stone artifacts is rapidly advancing Hawaiian archaeology due to the establishment of an energy dispersive X-ray fluorescence (EDXRF) laboratory at the University of Hawai'i at Hilo. Because EDXRF is non-destructive, it offers an unprecedented opportunity to infer the geographic origin of stone artifacts that might normally be off-limits for study due to their sacred nature or their value as artifacts (Kahn et al. 2009; Kirch et al. 2012; Lundblad et al. 2008; M. McCoy 2011; Mills et al. 2008; Mintmier 2007; Mintmier et al. 2012).

Although archaeology in Hawai'i offers intriguing insights on the consequences of contact and colonialism, it has only recently begun to receive sustained attention (e.g., Bayman 2008, 2010; Flexner 2010, 2012; Garland 1996; Kirch and Sahlins 1992; Klieger 1998; Lebo and Bayman 2001; Mills 2002a, 2009; Schuster 1992). However, archaeological studies of Hawaii's WWII Japanese internment camps, and Pearl Harbor and its related military environs, have received significant media attention. The archaeology of nineteenth- and twentieth-century sugarcane plantations is another area of research that has been well received by Hawaii's local multicultural community (Kraus-Friedberg 2011; Six 2005).

2

Seascapes and Landscapes

The eight main islands of the place known today as Hawai'i—from southeast to northwest: Hawai'i, Maui, Kaho'olawe, Lāna'i, Moloka'i, O'ahu, Kaua'i, and Ni'ihau—are together one of the most isolated land masses on the planet (Figure 2.1). Honolulu, the modern capital, is located 21° north of the equator, about the same latitude as Mexico City, and 158° west of the prime meridian, more than 3,200 km from the nearest continental landmass on the west coast of America. Modern jetliners make the trip between Honolulu and the West Coast cities of Los Angeles, San Francisco, and Seattle in five or six hours. Flights to Honolulu from cities in Asia on the other side of the Pacific Ocean take nearly twice as long. A modern sailboat makes the voyage to Honolulu from the West Coast in two to three weeks; the record for racing yachts in the TransPac race from Los Angeles to Honolulu has dropped from twelve days to five over the last century. The closest islands to the main islands are the so-called Northwest Hawaiian Islands, a group of rocks and atolls that stretches from Nihoa Island, 463 km northwest of Honolulu, to Holaniku (Kure Atoll), another 1,759 km beyond Nihoa. Kuaihelani (Midway Atoll), site of a fierce World War II battle, is near the northwest end of the chain. Remains of traditional Hawaiian settlements have been found on Nihoa and on Hā'ena (Necker Island), but have not been found or are absent farther up the chain.

All of these places—the American and Asian continents and the small islands of the Northwest Hawaiian Islands—played relatively peripheral roles in the history of the main Hawaiian Islands. Instead, the history of the islands is strongly tied to the homeland of the Hawaiian people in the Society and Marquesas Islands of Central Eastern Polynesia, some 3,400–4,000 km from Honolulu. The jetliner flight from Honolulu to Pape'ete in the Society Islands takes 5.5 hours today, about the same as a

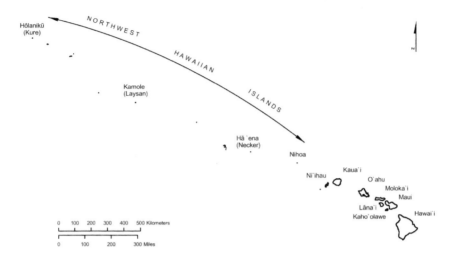

Figure 2.1: Map of the Hawaiian Islands. Northwest Hawaiian Island
names from Kikiloi (2010).

flight from Honolulu to the West Coast. Sailing between Hawai'i and the
homeland islands takes quite a bit longer than sailing to or from the West
Coast, however. The Hōkūle'a, a performance-accurate, full-size modern
replica of a traditional Polynesian voyaging canoe, makes the voyage using
traditional wayfinding techniques in about a month. One of the reasons for
the longer and more difficult voyage is the doldrums, the sailor's term for the
intertropical convergence zone, where the wind systems in the northern and
southern hemispheres come together near the equator to form a region of
baffling winds and heavy cloud cover. The native Hawaiian navigator
Nainoa Thompson, who practices traditional wayfinding techniques,
described his 1980 sail through the doldrums on Hōkūle'a as "a mess" (Public Broadcasting Service 1999). For long periods, he sailed blind as heavy
clouds blocked his view of the stars used for navigation, and when the winds
picked up they switched direction unpredictably, blowing the boat such that
it was difficult or impossible to track the canoe's path without instruments.

The Polynesian discovery of the isolated Hawaiian Islands was one of the
great achievements of its age, a triumph of skill and daring with few parallels
in human history. The islands discovered by the Polynesian seafarers were
quite a bit larger than those in the homeland (Table 2.1). Hawai'i Island,
which is larger than the other main Hawaiian Islands combined, is the third

Table 2.1: Island Areas in Hawai'i and Polynesia.

Group	Island	Area (km²)
New Zealand	South Island	151,215
New Zealand	North Island	113,729
Hawai'i	Hawai'i	10,433
Hawai'i	Maui	1,884
Samoa	Savai'i	1,694
Hawai'i	O'ahu	1,545
Hawai'i	Kaua'i	1,456
Society Islands	Tahiti	1,045
Hawai'i	Moloka'i	673
Hawai'i	Lāna'i	364
Marquesas	Nuku Hiva	339
Hawai'i	Kaho'olawe	116

largest island in all of Polynesia, smaller only than the North and South Islands of New Zealand. The next largest island in Polynesia outside Hawai'i is the Samoan Island of Savai'i, a namesake of Hawai'i, which ranks in size between Maui and O'ahu Islands. The largest island in the Eastern Polynesian homeland, Tahiti in the Society Islands, is about midway in size between Kaua'i and Moloka'i, the fourth and fifth largest Hawaiian islands, respectively. Nuku Hiva, the largest of the Marquesas Islands, another group in the East Polynesian homeland of Hawai'i, is roughly the size of Lāna'i Island, the sixth largest of the Hawaiian group.

Although the Hawaiian Islands as a group occupy an isolated spot in the North Pacific, the individual main islands are set relatively close to one another. It is possible to sail from one end of the main Hawaiian Islands to the other without losing sight of land. In fact, with the exception of O'ahu and Kaua'i, which are only intervisible in particular atmospheric conditions a few times a year, it is usually possible to see the next island or islands in the chain from a position on the shore. Thus, the sophisticated wayfinding techniques required to sail between Hawai'i and the homeland were not needed for inter-island trips within the main islands.

The northwest–southeast trend of the Hawaiian chain and the location of the main islands at the southeast end of the chain are both due to plate tectonics—in this case the movement of the ocean floor over a more or less stationary hot spot on the earth's crust where lava is extruded and islands are formed. The movement of the ocean floor over the hot spot is part of a process of seafloor spreading that starts at a long submarine ridge off the coast of the Americas known as the East Pacific Rise. The seafloor spreads both east and west from the rise. The eastern spread supplies the tectonic force that is creating the Andes, along with the Coast, Cascade, and Sierra Nevada ranges. The western spread moves the Pacific Plate about nine cm a year, the same rate at which a normal fingernail grows. This has created an age gradient along the Hawaiian chain, with the oldest islands at the northwest end and the youngest islands at the southwest end.

The islands at the northwest end of the Hawaiian chain, from Nihoa to Kuaihelani, were formed at the hot spot between 7 and 28 million years ago. Kaua'i and Ni'ihau, the northernmost of the main islands, were formed more than five million years ago. In contrast, Kīlauea Volcano, at the southern end of Hawai'i Island, is still active. The current phase of eruption there has been ongoing for the last 20 years. The submarine foundation for what might eventually be the next island in the chain is located about 45 km southeast of Hawai'i Island at a place that geologists have named Lo'ihi. The dormant Haleakalā Volcano on Maui and the Mauna Loa and Hualālai volcanoes on Hawai'i Island have all erupted since the islands were colonized by Polynesians. The most recent eruption at Haleakalā might have been as late as the eighteenth century and geologists believe it is likely to erupt in the next hundred years (Juvik and Juvik 1998:44). Hualālai last erupted early in the nineteenth century, creating new coastline and leaving behind vast tracts of dark lava still bare of vegetation. The last eruption at the summit of Mauna Loa was in 1984.

This age gradient is largely responsible for the great diversity in landforms across the Hawaiian Chain. The volcanic cores of the oldest islands in the Northwest Hawaiian Islands are either present as small remnants of erosion-resistant dike rock, as at Nihoa and Hā'ena, or have eroded beneath the sea, leaving behind coral rock atolls. In contrast, the main islands preserve evidence of more or less complex eruptive sequences at different stages of erosion. The older, northern islands of Kaua'i and O'ahu are deeply eroded. The Wailua River on Kaua'i is the only navigable river in the islands, and Pu'uloa on O'ahu, commonly known today as Pearl Harbor, was formed by the coalescence and flooding of three large valleys. Fringing reefs are well-developed at several of the northern islands and have provided plentiful material for the white sand beaches so successfully marketed by the tourist industry. Ironically, the most famous of these beaches at Waikīkī has too little sand of its own to be marketed successfully and has been supplemented

Figure 2.2: Snow near the summit of Mauna Kea, Hawai'i Island.

over the years by sand mined from beaches on the west end of Moloka'i Island and elsewhere.

The younger islands at the southeastern end of the chain are at a youthful erosional stage and rise high above the sea. The peak of Haleakalā Volcano on Maui stands just over 3,000 m above sea level and Mauna Kea and Mauna Loa on Hawai'i Island are each more than 3,962 m high. The tops of all three volcanoes are high enough to receive snowfall in the winter (Figure 2.2). Maui and Hawai'i are dissected by steep-sided valleys along their wet windward sides, but the drier leeward sides of these islands have just begun to be cut by intermittent streams. Reefs are not yet well-developed on these young islands, which have fewer and smaller sand beaches than their northern neighbors.

On both the younger and older islands of the chain, the shallow coastal waters and the mountainous island interiors served as primary reference points for orientation. The ubiquitous Hawaiian words *makai* and *mauka*, both formed with the indefinite locative *ma*, mean "toward the sea" and "toward the mountains," respectively. They establish local frames of reference independent of the points of a compass. Positions tangential to the ocean/mountain axis are typically indicated with reference to a local landmark. For example, in downtown Honolulu, directions to the southeast corner of a street intersection would typically use an appropriate local frame and refer instead to the *makai* Diamond Head corner of the intersection.

The climate of the islands is famously equable, with an annual variation of mean monthly temperatures less than the typical local daily range of 6–8°. The mountainous topography, however, creates a spatial diversity of climate unmatched almost anywhere else on earth. Local climates range from deserts to tropical rain forests—the wettest spot on earth, Mount Wai'ale'ale on Kaua'i Island, receives 1,143 cm of rain annually—to frozen alpine tundra on the formerly glaciated peak of Mauna Kea. The northeast trade winds that blow about 70 percent of the time bring moisture-laden air to the eastern sides of most islands. When this air rises over the mountains of the larger islands it cools and condenses, dropping rain before it passes to the drier lee sides. This orographic pattern distinguishes the wet windward sides of the larger islands from the drier leeward sides, a factor largely responsible for determining patterns of land use in traditional Hawai'i. The islands of Lāna'i and Kaho'olawe lie in the rain shadow of Haleakalā on neighboring Maui Island and lack the wet windward sides typical of the larger islands.

The geographic isolation of the islands makes it difficult for plants and animals to colonize them naturally, without human agency. In the marine environment this has resulted in a relatively depauperate marine flora and fauna derived primarily from the Indo-West Pacific, a region ranging from Indonesia to the Ryukyu Islands of southern Japan. Hawai'i has about 530 species of inshore bony fishes, compared with approximately 2,500 in the Philippines, and fewer than 800 species of marine molluscs compared with almost 2,500 species known from the Ryukyu Islands. There are a few notable absences—the Rabbitfishes (Siganidae), common farther west, are absent in Hawai'i, as are the chambered nautilus and the giant *Tridacna* clam (Ziegler 2002)—but the marine fauna as a whole is not disharmonic in an evolutionary sense, in that entire higher taxonomic groups that play major ecological roles are not absent (Ziegler 2002:122).

In contrast to the marine biota, the terrestrial and freshwater biota are diverse and unusual. Geographic isolation along with the topographic and climatic diversity of the terrestrial environment set the stage with a disharmonic biota that embarked on one of the most remarkable episodes of adaptive radiation in the history of the earth. The great diversity of terrestrial and freshwater plants and animals in Hawai'i includes many endemic species that evolved in Hawai'i and are, or were in the case of extinct species, found only in Hawai'i. Among flowering plants, 93 percent of broad-leafed plants are endemic and 69 percent of monocots, such as grasses, sedges, and palms, are endemic (Ziegler 2002:185). About 98 percent of the native insects, more than 95 percent of non-marine snails, and 82 percent of birds are endemic to Hawai'i (Ziegler 2002:203, 224, 253).

Studies of fossil pollen from paleoenvironmental cores and excavations indicate that many of the vegetation communities that evolved in Hawai'i prior to human colonization likely have no modern analogs. Lowland forests in which fantail palms (*Pritchardia* spp.) were a primary component, along with the shrub *Dodonaea viscosa*, are commonly recognized in the cores (Athens 1997; Athens et al. 2002:63; Burney et al. 2001:630–631). Modern lowland plant communities in which fantail palms are a dominant component are found only in remote localities—in two valleys on Nihoa Island in the Northwest Hawaiian Islands and on some of the world's tallest sea cliffs (Ziegler 2002:68) and an inaccessible islet on the windward coast of Moloka'i Island (Gagné and Cuddihy 1990:64). The understory in this forest commonly contained the now endangered *Kanaloa kahoolawensis*, a leguminous shrub known today in the wild from two individuals discovered in 1992 on an isolated seastack off Kaho'olawe Island (Athens 1997:256[14]; Lorence and Wood 1994), which lived on an equal footing with cheno-ams, *Chamaesyce*, and various sedges and grasses.

Unlike the plants, where fossil forms are confidently associated with living examples, much of the avian fauna that evolved in Hawai'i in pre-human times is known only through fossils, many of which have been discovered or collected by archaeologists working with other researchers, including paleontologists from the Smithsonian Institution. The disharmonic terrestrial fauna and the resulting process of adaptive radiation filled empty niches in sometimes unusual ways. For instance, the absence of a ground-dwelling mammalian herbivore left an empty niche that was filled in Hawai'i by ibises, ducks, geese, and rails that evolved flightlessness and, in some cases, powerful beaks (Ziegler 2002:277). The *moa nalo*, whose name is a recently coined term that means "lost fowl," descended from a mallard-like duck, but in its new niche grew to weights between 4.0 and 7.6 kg. A flightless goose known from fossils collected on Hawai'i Island stood 1.2 m tall and weighed approximately 8.6 kg (Ziegler 2002:258).

The ecological balance that was achieved in isolation proved fragile, with the result that human colonization and the introduction of plants and animals from the homeland initiated a period of radical environmental change, the traces of which can be clearly seen in archaeological and paleontological deposits that are reviewed in the following chapters.

3

Settlement and Chronology

Archaeologists in Hawai'i, like their colleagues elsewhere in the world, are keen to discover firsts. This desire manifests itself in Hawai'i as an intense interest in when Polynesians discovered and settled the Hawaiian Islands. This question has preoccupied Hawaiian archaeologists ever since the first ^{14}C date from Kuli'ou'ou shelter awakened them to the time depth of Hawaiian history. The story of how the question has been answered is thus a central theme in the practice of Hawaiian archaeology.

Like other Polynesians, Hawaiians reckoned historical time genealogically rather than with reference to an annual calendar. Attempts to interpret genealogies as calendric records and to estimate the date the Polynesian ancestors of the Hawaiians settled the islands began in the nineteenth century (see Kirch 2011). The genealogies tell of two waves of migration, where an earlier autochthonous people of the land were later colonized by a sea people who became their rulers, a historical motif with a wide distribution around the world (Sahlins 1981, 2008). Western reaction to the heroic histories based on traditions, such as Te Rangi Hiroa's classic evocation of his Polynesian ancestors as "Vikings of the sunrise" (Buck 1959), reached an extreme in the ideas of the historian Andrew Sharp who proposed that the Pacific had been settled by drift voyagers carried by currents and blown willy-nilly by the wind (Sharp 1963). Geographers soon demonstrated how unlikely it was that drift voyages were responsible for the settlement of Polynesia with an early computer simulation in which tables of wind and current information for the entire Pacific were laboriously entered into a mainframe computer with punch cards (Levison et al. 1973).

But it was the experiments carried out by the Polynesian Voyaging Society, founded in 1973 by anthropologist Ben Finney, Tommy Holmes, and Herb Kawainui Kane that answered the question of how Polynesia was settled.

Propelled into the public imagination by Kane's paintings of old Hawai'i and its voyaging canoes, the experiments culminated in 1976 with the voyage from Hawai'i to Tahiti of Hōkūle'a, a performance-accurate replica of a traditional Hawaiian double-hulled voyaging canoe, navigated without instruments by the Micronesian sailor and navigator Mau Pialug (Finney 1979). This and subsequent voyages navigated by Hawaiian students trained by Pialug left no doubt that Polynesians had the technical and cultural skills needed to explore vast stretches of ocean. It is sobering to realize that the Polynesian discoverers of Hawai'i had been sailing out of sight of land for at least a month when they made landfall, and that they were prepared for at least another month of landless sailing to return home in the event that no new lands were found (Irwin 1992).

The realization that archaeological excavation could contribute information that might help answer the question of when Hawai'i was settled came with the unexpectedly old age estimate returned by the first ^{14}C date from Hawai'i (Libby 1951). Initially, the ^{14}C method was seen as a scientific adjunct to the genealogies, capable of an objectivity and precision that the genealogies could not claim. Somewhat surprisingly to archaeologists, both objectivity and precision have proved elusive; settlement estimates based on ^{14}C dating evidence have produced a wider range than genealogical dating with its assumptions and uncertainties. Published estimates over the last two decades now range from the beginning of the Common Era (Hunt and Holsen 1991) to the thirteenth century A.D. (Wilmshurst et al. 2011).

Archaeologists have developed three different approaches to estimating when Polynesians settled Hawai'i: (i) searching for early sites; (ii) evaluating lists of ^{14}C dates compiled from site excavation reports; and (iii) evaluating ^{14}C dates from paleoenvironmental investigations. All of these approaches have been implemented in an ad hoc way, without benefit of an explicit chronological model.

Early ^{14}C-based estimates of the Polynesian settlement of Hawai'i were framed in the context of arguments for the ages of purportedly early sites on three islands. Arguments for an early establishment of three coastal sites were made, including Pu'u Ali'i, Site H1 on Hawai'i Island (Emory and Sinoto 1969); the Bellows dune, Site O18 on O'ahu Island (Pearson et al. 1971); and the Hālawa Valley Dune, Site MO-A1-3 on Moloka'i Island (Kirch and Kelly 1975), which was interpreted as somewhat later than the other two. At each of the three sites, artifactual or structural evidence was found that differed from expectations based on the known ethnographic and museum records and which was interpreted as indicating some antiquity for the site: at Puʻu Aliʻi this was a multi-faceted sequence of change in various types of fishing gear (Emory et al. 1968); at Bellows an artifact assemblage with an unusual shell coconut grater, pearl shell fishhooks, and adzes with trapezoidal and triangular cross sections (Pearson et al. 1971); and at Hālawa Valley, a buried round-ended house, untanged and ground adzes, and various early fishhook types (Kirch and Kelly 1975).

The early age estimate for each of these sites was subsequently challenged. Dye (1992) showed that the argument for an early date at Puʻu Aliʻi was based on outliers among the dated samples and he used an analysis of cumulative probability curves to argue for a much later fifteenth-century date for establishment of the site. The Bellows dune site was redated twice. The first attempt yielded somewhat equivocal results, which were interpreted as indicating a later establishment of the site in the eighth century A.D. (Tuggle and Spriggs 2001). The second attempt yielded a stratigraphically consistent set of results that compare favorably with other well-dated sites nearby and indicate that the site was established in A.D. 1040–1219, some nine centuries later than the earliest estimate of its age (Dye and Pantaleo 2010). Six new accelerator mass spectrometry (AMS) dates from contexts near the base of the Hālawa Dune site clearly indicate that the original estimate of the site's antiquity was based on an outlier, probably due to an "old wood effect" introduced by dating tree wood charcoal rather than short-lived material such as a twig, nutshell, or shrub (Bowman 1990; Taylor 1987). The Hālawa Dune site is now believed to have been established in the fifteenth century A.D. (Kirch and McCoy 2007).

This reassessment and questioning of putatively early sites as markers of settlement led in the 1990s to development of an approach that does not rely on identifying an early site. In this approach, a corpus of ^{14}C dates is assembled, the dates are calibrated, and the early tail of the temporal distribution of the calibrated ages is used to estimate the age of settlement. This is the approach used by Hunt and Holsen (1991) and Graves and Addison (1995) to argue that Hawaiʻi was discovered by Polynesians in the first to fifth centuries A.D. At the time these estimates were put forward, a settlement date in the first half of the first millennium appeared to be supported by the settlement sequence in the Eastern Polynesian homeland of Hawaiʻi. Subsequent ^{14}C dating of purportedly early sites there that controlled for the effects of old wood (Anderson and Sinoto 2002; Rolett and Conte 1995; Wilmshurst et al. 2008) has shown that the settlement sequence as it was understood in the early 1990s was several centuries too early. As a result, the estimated settlement ages for Hawai'i based on corpora of ^{14}C dates were recognized as implausibly early. In response to this situation, Wilmshurst et al. (2011) have developed a set of criteria for accepting or rejecting individual ^{14}C dates, based on their association with cultural activity, intrinsic sources of error, and the precision with which the dating laboratory measured the age of the sample, a variation on an approach known in the Pacific as "chronometric hygiene" (Spriggs and Anderson 1993). They have applied this approach to the problem of estimating the settlement dates of island groups in East Polynesia, including Hawai'i. Using a substantially reduced corpus of ^{14}C dates, this approach yields an estimate that Polynesian settlement of Hawai'i took place in A.D. 1219–1266. The method yields a similar result for the settlement of Hawai'i Island (Rieth et al. 2011). The method can be criticized for neglecting to relate the dated samples to the archaeological event of interest, and it yields estimates that are almost certainly too late (Dye 2011a).

A second response to the lack of early dated sites was to look outside of archaeological sites for information that might be used to infer when settlement took place (Burney et al. 2001; Athens et al. 2002). This approach yielded especially useful results on the 'Ewa Plain of O'ahu Island, where paleoenvironmental coring in Ordy Pond revealed a stratigraphic sequence of thin layers, each of which represents a short interval of time, and excavations in limestone sinkholes yielded apparently old materials introduced to the islands by Polynesians. Dates on materials from the pre-settlement and post-settlement periods were interpreted as supporting a settlement range of A.D. 700–800 (Athens et al. 2002:57, n. 1).

This approach has been extended using Bayesian techniques (Buck et al. 1996) to yield a model-based estimate of the settlement event (Dye 2011a). The Bayesian model establishes two periods, one for the period before the islands were settled by Polynesians and one for the period after the settlement event. Although ^{14}C dating material from pre-settlement period deposits is rarely, if ever, collected during archaeological excavations, it is routinely collected during paleoenvironmental coring on the older, northern islands of O'ahu and Kaua'i, which have consistently revealed a pattern of sediments with charcoal overlying sediments that lack charcoal. The charcoal in these cores has been attributed to human activities because, it is argued, the two causes of natural fires—volcanism and lightning strikes—were either absent or extremely rare on the northern islands. Paleoenvironmental coring investigations on Oʻahu Island at Ordy Pond yielded a finely divided stratigraphic profile with organic material from a charcoal-free stratum near the boundary marking the onset of charcoal deposition (Athens et al. 1999). ^{14}C dates from the post-settlement period are the oldest known on materials believed to have been introduced to the islands by Polynesians. These include a bone of the Polynesian rat, *Rattus exulans*; a nutshell of the *kukui* tree, *Aleurites moluccana*; a charred fragment of a tentatively identified sweet potato tuber, *Ipomoea batatas*; wood charcoal identified as breadfruit, *Artocarpus altilis*; a piece of gourd, *Lagenaria siceraria*; and wood charcoal identified as *kī, Cordyline fruticosa*. Barring the rather unlikely possibility that one or more of these dated specimens was brought to Hawaiʻi from the homeland by the first colonists, they cannot be older than the settlement event because they were unknown in Hawaiʻi during the pre-settlement period. They can be confidently assigned to the post-settlement period regardless of the archaeological contexts from which they derived.

The model and two data sets were calibrated with the BCal software package (Buck et al. 1999). The first data set used only post-settlement period dates on floral materials. It yielded a posterior probability of the settlement event with a 95 percent highest posterior density (HPD) region of A.D. 810–1289 and a mode at A.D. 980 (Figure 3.1, *left*). This estimate is relatively imprecise because the floral evidence for the early end of the post-settlement period is not strong. If the age of the oldest rat bone is added to the calibration, then the estimate of the settlement event has a 95 percent HPD region of A.D. 780–1119 with a mode at A.D. 960 (Figure 3.1, *right*).

The model-based estimate effectively solves the problem of when Hawaiʻi was settled by Polynesians by providing a logically coherent framework that can incorporate new data. Although the estimate yielded by the model, given current data, is not very precise, this will change as archaeologists date additional material from the pre-settlement and post-settlement periods.

The Hawaiian Archaeological Record

The practice of Hawaiian archaeology is dominated by the identification and description of surface architecture. Traditional Hawaiians were accomplished

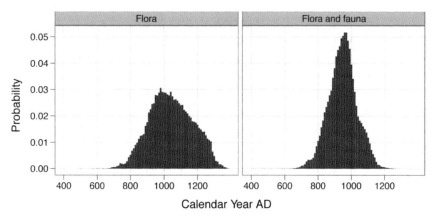

Figure 3.1: Posterior probability for Polynesian settlement of Hawai'i.
Left: estimate based on floral dates only, with a 95 percent highest posterior density
region of A.D. 810–1289. Right: posterior probability for Polynesian settlement
of Hawai'i, based on floral and faunal dates, with a 95 percent highest posterior
density region of A.D. 780–1119.

dry masons who used naturally occurring volcanic and sedimentary rock to create an archaeological landscape that is, in many places, dominated today by surface architectural remains. Abandoned, but otherwise undisturbed, Hawaiian settlements are often immediately visible, where they are not overgrown, and typically consist of a variety of stone structures—walls, terraces, platforms, enclosures, pavements, alignments, and mounds, together with a variety of paths, pits, ditches, and/or clearings. Description of surface architectural remains is one of the primary themes of Hawaiian archaeological reports, especially in the cultural resources management realm. Given this, it is unfortunate that archaeologists have not reached consensus on a set of descriptive terms for architecture or their application in the field, where the dilapidated condition of abandoned structures often complicates recording. In practice, one archaeologist's platform is another's terrace, etc., which greatly complicates efforts to synthesize and interpret the archaeological landscape.

Once described, architectural features are typically classified by archaeologists according to putative function, using broad categories such as "residential," "agricultural," "religious," or "special-purpose." In cultural resources management archaeology, this functional classification is a requirement of the inventory survey, where it is typically carried out largely on the basis of surface architectural form, impressionistically recorded, with little or no excavation. Early efforts to infer the past function of a structure with excavation (e.g., Kirch 1971; Takayama and Green 1970; Weisler and Kirch 1985) have not developed into standards that might be applied systematically and refined with experience.

Most of the residential features represent a fairly modest expenditure of construction effort, ranging from the foundations for obviously expedient structures typically less than about 20 m², to the more substantial structures typically smaller than 100 m² (Cordy et al. 1991:529). Much of the residential construction effort was spent on the perishable superstructure, typically a wooden pole frame lashed together with cord and thatched with grass, palm fronds, or the leaves of pandanus or ti plant (Apple 1971). Religious features also exhibit a wide range of sizes, from single upright stones without a perishable superstructure to relatively massive platforms divided into functionally specific areas and supporting several structures. One of the largest of these, Pi'ilanihale at Hāna, Maui Island, covers 12,126 m² (Kolb 1994, 2012). Perhaps the largest stone masonry structure built in traditional times is Kaneaka *hōlua* at Keauhou, Hawai'i, a stone slide nearly 1.6 km long where extreme athletes rode narrow wooden sleds at speeds that modern replication experiments indicate approached 40 mph.

The ubiquity of surface architecture, an obvious boon to archaeological investigation, has given it undue prominence in archaeological thought, to the point that Hawaiian archaeologists often conflate the definition of *surface architectural feature* and *site*. The archaeological definition of site is a *location* at which evidence of past human activity is preserved; one type of evidence of past human activity, among others, is surface architecture. In Hawai'i, however, the ubiquity of surface architecture and the great effort spent identifying and describing abandoned settlements has led archaeologists to define sites not as locations, but as surface architectural features. This semantic shift changes the way archaeologists view the relationship between architectural features and other evidence of past human activity at a site. Because archaeologists in Hawai'i typically consider a surface architectural feature to *be* a site, it is no longer viewed, as it should be, as evidence for typically late human activity *at* a site. Instead, this relation is turned on its head. Other evidence of past human activity at a site is viewed as an attribute of the surface architecture; investigation of that other evidence becomes, in the mind of the archaeologist, an extension of the initial project—the identification and description of surface architecture.

This type of confusion is part of a more general lack of concern with methodological issues in Hawaiian archaeology, such as the systematic description of surface architecture or the inference of function. The paradox here is that

> the practice of Hawaiian archaeology might seem quite simple because sites are relatively shallow, there is limited stratification, portable artifacts are few in number, and there is extensive surface architecture. But it is precisely these characteristics that make the practice of Hawaiian archaeology quite difficult. Without question there was a great deal of complexity and diversity in Hawaiian cultural behavior, but there is an enormous gap between that behavioral reality and the relative homogeneity of the archaeological landscape. (Tuggle 2010:159)

Tuggle (2010) argues that the perception of homogeneity is due, in part, to a failure to develop methods of description and inference that isolate axes of variability in the archaeological record. Instead of pursuing consensus on issues of systematics, Tuggle argues that Hawaiian archaeologists "find methodological comfort in being able to employ the richness of Hawaiian traditions in the island version of the direct historical approach to inference" (Tuggle 2010:160). For example, archaeologists who have been unable to find the conventional archaeological correlates of political economy in chiefdom or state societies typically turn to ethnohistoric records and traditional accounts to fill gaps in their narratives (e.g., Cordy 1981; Kirch 2010a).

Investigation of the Settlement Landscape

The ubiquity of surface architectural remains makes Hawai'i an ideal location to investigate patterns of settlement. As we noted in Chapter 1, the settlement pattern approach was introduced to Hawai'i by the late Roger Green (Green 1984) and the approach remains a dominant focus of research today.

The territorial divisions of the islands were recorded in detail in the mid-nineteenth century, some 70 years after Cook's visit initiated sustained contact with the non-Polynesian world. At that time, each of the islands was divided into nested, named territories. The fundamental territory was the *ahupua'a*, which typically included both land and shallow nearshore waters (Figure 3.2). The *ahupua'a* and its residents constituted the unit that paid tribute in the form of consumables, wealth items, and services. On the

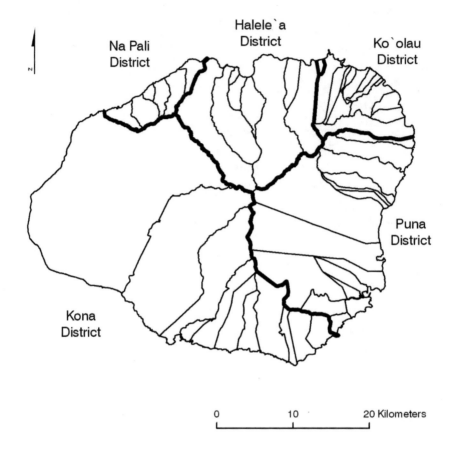

Figure 3.2: Territorial Divisions of Kaua'i Island in the Early Historic Period.
Note: The divisions of districts are *ahupua'a*.

windward sides of all islands and the well-dissected leeward sides of the older islands, *ahupua'a* boundaries on land were typically coincident with a drainage basin that debauched to the sea. On the undissected lands of the younger islands, the boundaries of *ahupua'a* were not determined by topography, but even here were long and often narrow like a river valley and typically stretched from the nearshore waters up into the mountains. In a common pattern, the highest elevations of the larger islands were the territory of a relatively few *ahupua'a*, which expanded as they moved up the mountains, cutting off other *ahupua'a* in the process. There were various subdivisions of *ahupua'a*, most commonly the *'ili* lands associated with residential groups, but many others, as well. On the larger islands, groups of about 30 or more *ahupua'a* comprised named districts, or *moku*, each of which was ruled by its own chief.

A model for development of the settlement hierarchy based on archaeological and other data was set out by Hommon (1986). The earliest small settlements were sparsely distributed along the coasts of all the major islands in ecologically favorable locations, so-called salubrious cores (Hommon 1986), separated from one another by relatively inhospitable buffer zones in a pattern reminiscent of contact-era *moku*. These early settlements expanded inland with the development of large-scale permanent agricultural facilities, creating the coastal-inland axis that was later fundamental to the *ahupua'a* land unit. Subsequently, populations outgrew the production potential of the salubrious cores and their inland agricultural fields, leading to expansion of settlement laterally into former buffer zones of more limited agricultural potential. When this was accomplished, the pattern of settlement that is described in contact-period documentary accounts and presumably reflected in the archaeological landscape was in place.

The known distribution of surface architectural features and sites on Hawai'i, using information compiled by the State Historic Preservation Division until 2005, is shown on Figure 3.3. The patchy distribution of sites evident on the figure is due to several factors.

The concentration of sites along the coast in each of the districts reflects traditional Hawaiian patterns of activity, with their focus on the ocean, and the intensity of CRM archaeology carried out in advance of the explosion of coastal development since the late 1960s. In contrast, the mountainous interior of the island was used less intensively in traditional Hawaiian times and remains largely undeveloped today. The large cluster of sites in the interior of Hāmākua District represents the Mauna Kea adze quarry, where outcrops of lava extruded beneath the glaciated cap of the mountain in the Pleistocene yielded a fine-grained, tabular rock ideal for production of stone adzes. Many of the other upland sites in and near Hāmākua District represent shelters used by bird hunters.

Land development prior to passage of historic preservation laws is responsible for the smaller number of sites on the east side of the island. The Hāmākua, Hilo, and Puna districts on the wet windward side of the island are rich agricultural lands that were planted in sugarcane for most of the

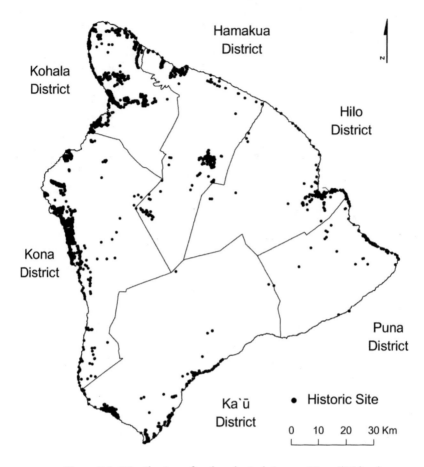

Figure 3.3: Distribution of archaeological sites on Hawai'i Island.

nineteenth and twentieth centuries. With the possible exception of the narrow gulches that drain this coast, which have been only partially explored, the archaeological record here has been virtually erased by deep steam plows employed by the sugar planters.

On the drier, western side of the island the site distribution in the Kohala and northern Kona districts shows the traditional pattern of coastal fishing and inland agricultural settlements separated by a dry, inhospitable "barren zone." The more compact and dense distribution of sites in the heart of the Kona District is an area where the agricultural lands extended down to the coast, which looks out on some of the richest fishing grounds in the islands.

The sparse distribution of sites south of here and through Ka'u District reflects primarily the lack of land development in these still rural areas.

Hawaiian archaeologists often assume that this settlement landscape was built up by accretion over the course of Hawaiian prehistory, and that structures representing the full sequence of occupation are present today. However, archaeologically determined construction dates for habitation structures indicate that much of the extant surface architecture is late, and that a range of ages consistent with the accretion model is not evident. These findings have led to a recent hypothesis that the use lives of dry stone masonry habitation foundations were tied to the use lives of the pole-and-thatch structures built on and within them, and that they were rebuilt periodically, the stones from an old foundation salvaged for use on a new foundation nearby (Dye 2010).

At the same time, construction dates on religious structures indicate a range of ages consistent with fixed locations over long periods of time, consistent with excavation results that demonstrate multiple reconstruction events (e.g., Kolb 1991; Ladd 1973). This observation has given rise to the hypothesis that there are two components to the diachronic settlement pattern of traditional Hawai'i, with a relatively fixed set of temple structure locations surrounded by a more transient set of habitation structures (Dye 2010). Over time, the structures of individual temples might change as old structures were repaired and remodeled, and new temple structures might be built. But, once built, the locations of temples would not change and their spatial relations to one another would stay the same. In contrast, the pattern of habitation structures almost certainly involved changes in location as old structures were abandoned and then dismantled for the materials needed to build new habitations nearby.

Chronological Issues

One result of the redating of the Bellows dune and Hālawa Dune sites and the reinterpretation of the age of the Pu'u Ali'i site is that the cultural sequence established in the 1980s, and used by most archaeologists since then, is in tatters. That sequence established five periods: a Colonization Period, A.D. 300–600; a Developmental Period, A.D. 600–1100; an Expansion Period, A.D. 1100–1650; a Proto-Historic Period, A.D. 1650–1795; and a Historic Period leading to modern times (Kirch 1985:298ff.). It is now clear that the Colonization Period is too early by several centuries and that most of the subsequent Developmental Period refers to a time before Polynesians discovered the islands. What once seemed to be a reasonable sequence of cultural development now appears to reflect the vicissitudes of selecting unsuitable materials for ^{14}C dating and an ad hoc approach to interpretation, rather than reflecting what actually happened in old Hawai'i.

One response to this has been to concentrate on events of the latter part of the sequence and to rely more heavily on comparative ethnography and interpretations of oral traditions for inferring past behavior and chronology (Kirch 2010a). This is certainly a reasonable tactic, but archaeologists will want to adopt a strategy that re-establishes an archaeological sequence. This strategy will require greater attention to ^{14}C dating issues in future excavations and most probably continued redating of excavated sites with important collections. This work is currently in an early stage and a revised archaeological sequence has not been proposed. It is useful, however, to see what has been achieved, both for its substantive results and for an indication of what is left to be done.

An initial step has been taken by Wilmshurst et al. (2011) and by Rieth et al. (2011), who have assessed potential sources of error in large sets of ^{14}C dates from Hawai'i and elsewhere in the Pacific, with the goal of estimating when Polynesians settled Hawai'i. This work indicates how thoroughly efforts to construct archaeological chronologies have been hampered by the long tradition of dating unidentified wood charcoal: suitable materials make up less than 13 percent of the total from Hawai'i Island (Rieth et al. 2011) and less than seven percent of the total from the entire group (Wilmshurst et al. 2011). Although the ad hoc interpretive methods used by these authors failed to achieve a useful estimate of the settlement event (Dye 2011a), and their particular brand of "chronometric hygiene" confuses accuracy and precision, which leads them to reject imprecise dates whose accuracy is not in question, the resulting compilations and assessments of ^{14}C dates provide a useful starting point for chronology building. The compilations are available electronically, and it is a relatively easy matter to identify dates on suitable materials for analysis.

The association of dated events and target events, which is fundamental to successful application of the ^{14}C dating method, is often honored in the breach by Hawaiian archaeologists. It is useful, however, to consider what archaeological events have been dated with suitable materials and the temporal distributions of the different classes of events. This exercise often requires that the archaeological event be inferred from a description of the context of the find, which is potentially error-prone when it is not done by the excavator. Still, the exercise is useful because it can indicate constraints on the kinds of questions that can be addressed with archaeological data that are available and point to areas where data collection might be directed in the future.

Many of the oldest ^{14}C age determinations are on secondarily deposited materials or pieces of charcoal found scattered through the soil matrix and not associated with an archaeological feature. This is the case for the oldest materials from the Bellows dune site on Oʻahu Island (Dye 2011a) and the old dates on dispersed charcoal from Wailau Valley (McElroy 2007) and from Kaupikiawa rockshelter (Kirch et al. 2003) on Molokaʻi Island, and from the Leeward Kohala agricultural field system on Hawaiʻi Island (Ladefoged and Graves 2008). The most that can be said about the archaeological events that created these pieces of charcoal is that they were cultural, rather than natural, burning events. The dated materials are not stratigraphically associated with artifacts or food remains whose analysis might support more detailed behavioral inferences.

None of the well-dated habitation sites have yielded artifact assemblages that characterize the nature of early Polynesian settlement. There is no published record of the artifacts and food remains associated with the early firepit features from sites on the Pololū Valley dune on Hawaiʻi Island (Field and Graves 2008; Tuggle and Tomonari-Tuggle 1980). Both Layer III at the Bellows dune site on Oʻahu Island (Dye and Pantaleo 2010:116) and the lower sector of Layer IV at the Hālawa Dune Site on Molokaʻi Island (Kirch and McCoy 2007) yielded early dates, but both deposits also yielded much later ^{14}C dates that indicate that these "early" layers were deposited over a period of several centuries. It is not possible, on stratigraphic grounds, to isolate the early artifact types that might be present in these deposits.

The cultural deposits with early dates are all buried in marine sand at the mouths of valleys. The structural remains that are present, such as fire pits, the remains of pavements, or the round-ended house foundation at Hālawa Valley, have no surface expression. The earliest well-dated surface architectural features are temple structures from ʻAlae Iki, Maui, which was constructed sometime after A.D. 1380 (Dye 2010:131); Hāpaialiʻi Heiau at Kahaluʻu, Hawaiʻi Island, which was constructed in A.D. 1369–1496 (Dye 2010:140); and KAL-1 at Kālala on the leeward Kohala coast of Hawaiʻi

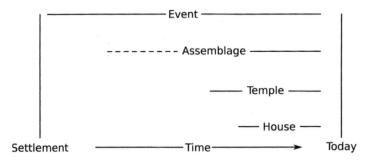

Figure 3.4: Temporal distribution of well-dated archaeological events.

Island (Field et al. 2010). All of these early surface architectural features were constructed in the last half of the traditional Hawaiian sequence.

The surface remains of habitation sites appear to be younger still. Well-dated construction events for habitation sites date to the late seventeenth and eighteenth centuries (Dye 2010:132). Claims for older habitation structures are typically based on ^{14}C dates that are not stratigraphically associated with surface architecture and are unlikely to yield information on construction events (e.g., Field et al. 2011:Table 1).

This review of the well-dated materials available for constructing a culture-historical chronology is summarized in Figure 3.4, which indicates the general temporal pattern rather than a precise chronology. The archaeological evidence for the first half of the traditional Hawaiian period, from the time of initial settlement up through the fourteenth century, is extremely slim. The burning events recovered from several sites indicate human activity and help to establish a settlement date, but carry little other behavioral information. Early assemblages of artifacts and food remains, indicated on the figure with a dashed line, are either not reported or come from deposits that accumulated over extended periods, effectively mixing the early materials with materials from the later part of the sequence. Surface architectural remains, whose identification and description is a particular preoccupation of Hawaiian archaeologists, appear to have been constructed relatively late in traditional Hawaiian times.

The obvious conclusion from this review of the temporal distribution of well-dated archaeological events is that careful excavation of early deposits is required before archaeological remains shed light on the first half of the traditional Hawaiian sequence. Some clarity might be gained by re-dating potentially early sites if suitable dating materials from appropriate contexts can be identified in collections. A good candidate for this type of project might be the H8 site at Wai'ahukini on Hawai'i Island, which yielded a large artifact assemblage from a well-stratified deposit (Emory et al. 1969). Other sites that have yielded early dates, such as the Pololū Dune, might be re-excavated with the goal of recovering larger assemblages of cultural materials from deposits of relatively short duration. Until this work is accomplished, the range and temporal scope of inferences about old Hawai'i based on archaeological materials will remain extremely limited, a poor guide to the behavioral richness and change indicated by comparative ethnography and Hawaiian tradition. An accurate chronology with well-dated artifact assemblages from each part of the sequence is vital for interpreting the pace of political change and the development of complex chiefdoms and states in ancient Hawai'i.

4

Food Production Economy

The epic "voyages of rediscovery" carried out by Hōkūle'a fixed public attention on the challenges of wayfinding and seamanship that were overcome by Polynesian colonists of Hawai'i. Having discovered new islands far from the homeland, colonists faced the daunting task of establishing viable communities capable of reproducing themselves in substantial isolation. This task was every bit as difficult as the voyage from the homeland. The islands in their natural state produced none of the plants that Polynesians depended upon for their staple starches, and the native forests that they found, which stretched from near the shore to the tops of the smaller islands and to the tree-lines of Maui and Hawai'i Islands, contained "no plants suitable as dietary staples" (Abbott 1992:6). It seems likely that the colonists initially relied on the marine environment for food and that they preyed on nesting colonies of seabirds and marine turtles like their ancestors did when they discovered and settled other islands in Polynesia. Excavations at colonization-era sites elsewhere in Polynesia document a diet rich in seabirds, turtles, and other marine life, but sites similar to these haven't been reported from Hawai'i (Dye and Steadman 1990). Regardless of whether the first colonists exploited large colonies of turtles and seabirds, or simply relied on the bountiful products of the nearshore marine environment for initial support, the long-term success of the new Polynesian colonies depended upon successful transfer of crop plants and domestic animals from the homeland and their establishment in Hawai'i. The geographer Edgar Anderson expressed the character of this process by the term "transported landscape," (Kirch 1982b) which gets neatly at the scope of a project that transformed the natural environment described in Chapter 2 to a cultural landscape capable of sustaining a large population.

Introduction of Plants and Animals

Biologists have established a list of the plants and animals successfully transported to and established on the islands of Hawai'i by Polynesians (Table 4.1). Many of the introduced plants were food plants, including the staple starches of the typical carbohydrate-rich Polynesian diet: taro, the primary staple in Hawai'i, typically cooked, pounded and mixed with a bit of water to make *poi*; breadfruit, the object of William Bligh's mutinous *Bounty* voyage to Tahiti, vast groves of which were established in the Kona District of Hawai'i Island; banana, typically eaten green before its starches have turned to sugars; sweet potato, introduced to the Pacific from South America, unlike most other crops with origins in Southeast Asia; elephant's ear, whose irritating tuber was used by Hawaiians primarily as a famine food; and the true yams of the genus *Dioscorea*, grown primarily on the northern island of Ni'ihau at the time of European contact and much sought after by Cook and other seamen because they can be stored for several months without loss of quality. The other three plants listed as foods in Figure 4.1 include coconut, which appears to have been less prevalent in Hawai'i than elsewhere in Polynesia, but also supplied leaves for plaiting and sennit for cordage; sugarcane, a sweet snack and also a common agricultural field border and windscreen; and arrowroot, made into a starch for thickening puddings.

The three domesticated animals introduced for food were pigs, dogs, and chickens. The pigs, somewhat smaller than European hogs, were by far the most important of the three by the time of European contact. A contact-era taboo on their consumption by women and their importance in rituals were factors in the large herd sizes noted by the first Europeans at the islands. According to tradition upwards of 2,000 pigs might be sacrificed at the consecration of a major religious temple (Malo 1996:252). Cook's ships found a bountiful supply and at times, according to Charles Clerke, who assumed command after Cook's death, the "Natives bring onboard so many Hogs we know not what to do with them" (Beaglehole 1967:576). Dogs, also taboo to women, and chickens appear to have played a smaller role.

Some plants were introduced for qualities other than food value. Kava, a soporific narcotic that typically produces a mild euphoria and relaxation, was used for recreation and ritual. Leaves of the ti plant were used to wrap food cooked in earth ovens. The candlenut tree, whose oily nuts fueled lamps, is

Table 4.1: Plants and Animals Introduced to Hawai'i by Polynesians.

Species	English	Hawaiian	Use
Staple starches			
Alocasia macrorrhiza	elephant's ear	*'ape*	food
Colocasia esculenta	taro	*kalo*	food
Ipomoea batatas	sweet potato	*'uala*	food
Dioscorea alata	greater yam	*uhi*	food
Dioscorea bulbifera	bitter yam	*hoi*	food
Dioscorea pentaphyllum	edible yam	*pi'a*	food
Artocarpus altilis	breadfruit	*'ulu*	food
Musa spp.	banana	*mai'a*	food
Other food plants			
Cocos nucifera	coconut	*niu*	food
Saccharum officinarum	sugarcane	*kō*	food
Tacca leontopetaloides	arrowroot	*pia*	food
Syzigium malaccense	mountain apple	*'ōhi'a 'ai*	food
Animals			
Sus scrofa	pig	*pua'a*	food
Canis familiaris	dog	*'īlio*	food
Gallus gallus	chicken	*moa*	food
Rattus exulans	Polynesian rat	*'iole*	?
Useful plants			
Piper methysticum	kava	*'awa*	narcotic
Cordyline fruticosa	ti	*kī*	packaging
Aleurites moluccana	candlenut	*kukui*	torch
Lagenaria siceraria	bottle gourd	*ipu*	container
Thespesia populnea	milo	*milo*	wood
Broussonetia papyrifera	paper mulberry	*wauke*	cloth
Heteropogon contortus	twisted beardgrass	*pili*	thatch
Schizostachyum glaucifolium	bamboo	*'ohe*	construction
Morinda citrifolia	Indian mulberry	*noni*	medicine
Cordia subcordata	kou	*kou*	wood

found today in small hanging valleys where it is unlikely to have established itself naturally. It appears that nuts were deliberately sown to facilitate the spread of a useful tree (Ziegler 2002:330–331). The bottle gourd, perhaps a native of South America like the sweet potato (Clarke et al. 2006), was dried and used as a calabash. The inner bark of the paper mulberry provided the material from which barkcloth was made, and its relative, the Indian mulberry, produces a fruit that was put to medicinal use. The *milo* tree, bamboo, and twisted beardgrass appear to have been introduced for building materials, and the *kou* tree, which is not especially useful otherwise, might have been introduced as a favored element of village landscaping.

Hawaiian tradition recalls that the plants and animals in this transported landscape were not all introduced at once, but instead came to the islands over a period of some centuries. The sequence of introductions is still being worked out archaeologically, but the results to date indicate that there were at least two waves of introductions, one early in the sequence and a second some 300–400 years later (Dye 2011a:135). On present evidence, the first wave included the candlenut tree and the Polynesian rat. Candlenuts are an obvious choice for provisioning a voyage of discovery. They are small, sturdy, almost certain to germinate after a long sea voyage, and would have been useful as torches during the voyage (Abbott 1992:5). It would have been advantageous to plant them in advance of subsequent colonizing voyages; later colonists could harvest candlenuts immediately rather than waiting for saplings to mature and bear nuts.

In contrast to the candlenut tree, the Polynesian rat had what appears to be an immediate and large effect on the native forest, leading to what archaeologists have characterized as the catastrophic disappearance of the native lowland forest (Athens 2008). The evidence for the early effects of rats comes from the finely stratified paleoenvironmental record at Ordy Pond where the pollen of native forest species begins to decline before charcoal is found in the sediments, the charcoal being evidence for burning that is expected when Polynesians modify the landscape. Three major contributors to the pollen record of the pre-colonization period begin their decline at this time—the *Pritchardia* palm, a shrub-tree *Dodonaea* sp., and the nearly extinct shrub *Kanaloa kahoolawensis*, which was known to science only by its pollen until a single individual was recently discovered on a sea stack near Kahoʻolawe Island (Lorence and Wood 1994). Their place in the pollen record was taken by herbs and grasses (Athens et al. 2002:Fig. 4), suggesting that the introduction of rats brought about a change in the structure of the forest, with a diminution of canopy and understory that opened up the forest and allowed herbs to flourish.

The introduction of Polynesian rats appears also to have been a factor in the extinction of the larger flightless birds (Athens et al. 2002). These birds, which evolved flightlessness to occupy an empty niche, could not compete with the new ground-dwelling omnivore. It is not clear what direct role humans might have played in this process. Archaeologists in Hawaiʻi have found no evidence comparable to the *moa* ovens of the New Zealand Maori (e.g., Anderson 1989) that might indicate that the Polynesian colonists of Hawai'i played a direct role in these extinctions, though it is hard to imagine that big flightless birds were not easy and desirable prey. Perhaps the absence of *moa* ovens in Hawai'i is a symptom of the hiatus between colonization and the first archaeological evidence of settlement, or alternatively an indication that humans colonized the islands episodically at first, giving the Polynesian rat time to modify the pristine ecosystem and drive the large flightless birds to extinction before human colonies were well established. In any event, it seems certain that the extraordinary fecundity of Polynesian rats, which would have enabled them to reach carrying capacity in a decade or two, let them substantially transform the pristine environments that humans would later occupy and develop.

Hawaiian tradition recalls and archaeological evidence indicates that several plants were introduced to Hawai'i subsequent to colonization. Breadfruit (Allen 2004:215–216; Allen and Murakami 1999; Handy and Handy 1972:149–155; McCoy et al. 2010) and kava (Lebot et al. 1992), whose thirteen unique Hawaiian cultivars are somatic mutations from a single variety (Lebot et al. 1999), are both propagated vegetatively and were thus likely to pose a challenge to long-distance sea transport. In contrast, the late arrivals of sweet potato and perhaps bottle gourd (Clarke et al. 2006) were likely due to the fact that both of these plants originated in South America and were not present in the homeland when Hawai'i was settled. At issue here are the nature and timing of contacts between Eastern Polynesia and South America (Álvaro Montenegro et al. 2008; Fitzpatrick and Callaghan 2009; Green 2005). Green (2000, 2005) reviewed a variety of evidence and concluded that sweet potato and bottle gourd were introduced to Eastern Polynesia in the eleventh to twelfth centuries A.D., some centuries after Hawai'i was discovered by Polynesians. Dated evidence of contact between Eastern Polynesia and South America, which might be associated with transfer of the two plants, has been claimed for chicken bones from the site of El Arenal-1 on the coast of south-central Chile where analysis of mtDNA indicates a probable Polynesian genetic signature for archaeological bones dated to A.D. 1304–1424 (Storey et al. 2007; but see Fitzpatrick and Callaghan 2009; Gongora et al. 2008). Archaeological evidence indicates that the sweet potato was introduced to Hawai'i by A.D. 1300–1419 (Ladefoged et al. 2005) and that the bottle gourd was introduced by A.D. 1280–1409

(Williams 2002). Thus, on present evidence, the process of transporting a Polynesian landscape to Hawai'i was a dynamic one that responded to changes in the homeland landscape over a period of three to five centuries.

Agricultural Development

The development of traditional Hawaiian agriculture plays a prominent role in archaeological theories of social change. Timothy Earle's study of the design and layout of irrigation systems on the north coast of Kaua'i Island evaluated three theories of cultural evolution, among them the hydraulic theory of Wittfogel (1957), the managerial benefits theory of Service (1962), and the warfare theory of Carneiro (1970). He found all of them unable to explain the Hawaiian case: (i) there was "virtually no evidence that Hawaiian irrigation would have required centralized management, construction, maintenance, or water distribution" (Earle 1978:193–194); (ii) the self-sufficient *ahupua'a* land unit was evidence that there was little or no environmentally determined specialization of local communities that might lead to creation of a redistributional economy; and (iii) Hawaiian warfare was not a result of competition over subsistence resources. Instead, he theorized that Hawaiian chiefs exercised authority through control over access to irrigation facilities and their products, a strategy he calls staple finance (e.g., Earle 1997).

Other theorists have found support for the ideas of Wittfogel and Carneiro. Support for the hydraulic theory has come from excavations of agricultural terraces on the windward side of O'ahu Island, which found evidence interpreted as "standardized pondfield construction techniques and coordinated water use" (Allen 1991:122) emblematic of "direct control at a supralocal level, manifested as a standardized technology" (Allen 1991:125). Robert Hommon has developed the idea that warfare was central to the development of the traditional Hawaiian states and that it was a result of competition over limited agricultural lands (Hommon 1986, 2010). Kirch (1994, 2010a) finds the root cause of traditional Hawaiian political dynamics in the contrasting properties of irrigated and rain-fed agricultural systems, with the relative uncertainties and fluctuations of yield in rain-fed agricultural systems the cause of wars being fought over productive resources.

There is a long history of investigation into the development of agriculture in traditional Hawai'i. Functional descriptions of post-contact agricultural systems began to be synthesized in the 1930s (Handy 1940; Handy and Handy 1972). Many of these systems were modern versions of traditional facilities and the functional descriptions have provided a strong foundation for archaeological work. Archaeologists have contributed substantially to the documentation and explanation of the spatial distribution of agriculture with detailed descriptions of individual systems and a series of regional distribution maps. Much less progress has been made working out the chronology of agricultural development and there are various interpretations of most dating results.

A signal accomplishment of Hawaiian archaeology was the recent publication of a map showing the distribution of traditional Hawaiian irrigated and rain-fed agricultural fields across the main Hawaiian Islands (Ladefoged et al. 2009) (Figure 4.1). Unlike earlier distribution maps (e.g., Earle 1980; Newman 1970), this map is not based on the records archaeologists and ethnologists have made of agricultural fields, but was constructed instead using a geographic information system database of environmental characteristics and a set of queries based largely on the results of investigations carried out as part of the multi-disciplinary Hawai'i Biocomplexity Project (Hawai'i Biocomplexity Project Team 2010). The predictive maps have been shown to fit the known distribution of irrigated and rain-fed agricultural fields and to predict where others, as yet not investigated archaeologically but some visible in aerial imagery, will be found (Ladefoged et al. 2010).

Among other contributions, the predictive maps have given precision to a long-held impression that traditional agricultural opportunities were distributed unequally among the main Hawaiian Islands. Irrigated agriculture of taro played a much more substantial role in the older, dissected islands, while rain-fed agriculture based on sweet potato was primarily carried out on younger soils on Maui and Hawai'i Islands. Suitable conditions for irrigated agriculture were found in valleys throughout Kaua'i and O'ahu, on the east end of Moloka'i, the west end of Maui, along the north and to a lesser extent southeast coasts of east Maui, and in gulches and valleys along the windward coast of Hawai'i Island. Areas with a high potential for rain-fed agriculture are:

- absent on Kaua'i;
- on O'ahu found on colluvial lands along the south coast east of Pearl Harbor, much of the east end, and scattered spots along the windward coast to the northern tip of the island;

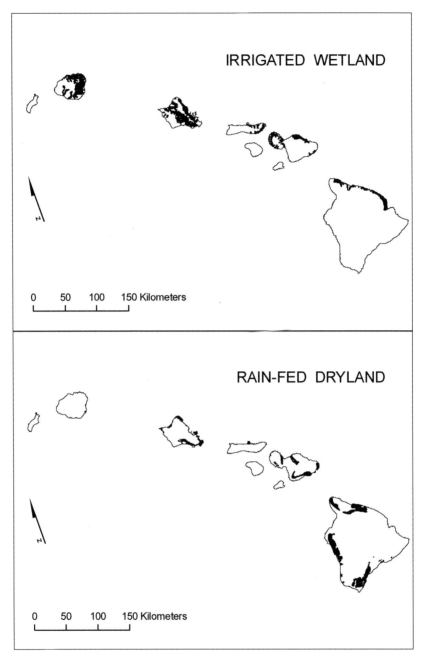

Figure 4.1: Predicted distributions of irrigated and rain-fed agricultural fields.
Source: Ladefoged et al. (2010).

- located on the geologically young Kalaupapa Peninsula on the north coast of Molokaʻi;
- situated on a band of colluvial soils on the windward side of west Maui, and at three areas on east Maui—a strip running inland on the north coast, at the east end, and a long strip some distance inland from and parallel to the south coast;
- distributed across four large areas of Hawaiʻi Island, including the Leeward Kohala field system in the north, a portion of the windward coast leading inland to the modern town of Waimea, the Kona field system of the west coast, and a large swath of the southern portion of the island centered on the eastern coast.

Wet weight production estimates indicate the magnitude of the disparities and their geographic distribution. Moving from the younger islands in the south to the older islands in the north, production from irrigated fields is estimated at 12 percent of the yield on Hawaiʻi, 50 percent on Maui, 86 percent on Molokaʻi, 93 percent on Oʻahu, and 100 percent on Kauaʻi (Figure 4.2).

Taro Pondfields

Production of taro in irrigated pondfields represents one apogee of traditional Hawaiian agriculture. In the early twentieth century, several generations after the introduction of a Western property rights regime deprived most native Hawaiians of their access to irrigated pondfields, it was still possible for an ethnologist to collect 342 names of taro varieties. The irrigated pondfields were extremely productive, yielding an estimated 25 metric tons per hectare annually (Kirch 1994; Spriggs and Kirch 1992), about five times the yield typically attained in rain-fed fields where sweet potato was the primary crop. Water drawn into the pondfields from streams provided a rich source of nutrients for the taro plants, which grew to maturity in six to nine months.

An island-wide survey of taro pondfields in the 1930s (Handy 1940) has been followed up more recently by detailed regional studies (e.g., Allen 1987; Allen et al. 2002; Earle 1978; Field and Graves 2008; McElroy 2007; Riley 1975; Tuggle and Tomonari-Tuggle 1980; Yen et al. 1972).

A classification of pondfield systems according to water source and bund construction encompasses their formal variability (Kirch 1977:260).

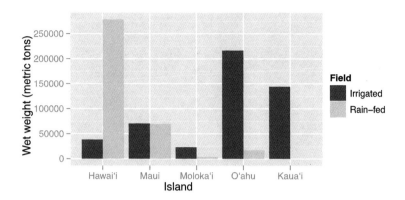

Figure 4.2: Agricultural production estimates for irrigated and rain-fed agricultural fields. Source: Ladefoged et al. (2010).

- At the simple end are narrow channel barrage systems in which a series of low walls in intermittent stream beds served to trap sediment and impound water.
- Single ditch, direct feed systems consist of a short ditch that feeds water to a small series of pondfields constructed on an alluvial flat. The individual pondfields of these systems typically consist of a stone-faced bund behind which is a flat surface that is flooded during cropping (Figure 4.3). Water flowed into the top of the system at a single point and flowed from one field to another before spilling onto the ground from the lowest field(s). The number of pondfields in systems of this type ranged from about 10 to 40, and the system typically produced enough food for about two to 12 people.
- Peripheral ditch, multiple feed systems are found on larger alluvial flats. A ditch brings water off the stream and runs along the base of the valley wall, feeding at several points into a system of pondfields typically with stone-faced bunds. In these systems, the water ran from one pondfield to the next back toward the stream and simply spilled out onto the ground after it exited the system. Systems of this type might have several dozen pondfields and produce enough food for two to three dozen people.
- The most complex systems, typically located on the largest alluvial flats near the coast, have multiple ditches and are configured like nested peripheral ditch systems, with the added feature that water from outer

Figure 4.3: An abandoned single-ditch, direct-feed
pondfield system at Mānoa, Kauaʻi.

parts of the system is reclaimed by inner ditches that add it to the water
they pull from the stream and redistribute to their portion of the system.
In these systems, some of the pondfield bunds might be earthen and others stone-faced. Systems of this type can contain hundreds of pondfields
and produce enough food for several hundred people.

Within abandoned pondfield systems, the flow of irrigation water can be
reconstructed using detailed observations on "canal bifurcations and
arrangements of spillways, embankments, tunnels, and other structures that
regulated water distribution" (Spriggs and Kirch 1992:138), and this information can be used to divide a pondfield system into subsystems of shared
water sources. This research strategy is useful for pondfield subsystems that
were in use during the historic period because they can be associated with
cultivators whose names appear in land records. Because the land records
sometimes record the relationships of cultivators to one another, it is possible to work out the "social relations of irrigation" (Spriggs and Kirch
1992:154), where the flow of water, a source of wealth, links and orders various social categories. These methods developed for use in the historic period
might be usefully generalized and applied to pondfields that are not
described in the historic record.

Excavations in pondfields reveal stratigraphic profiles where the pondfield soils can be distinguished by an illuvial B-horizon with red ferruginous mottling, charcoal flecking, and the presence of tubular limonite concretions that apparently formed around taro roots (Kirch 1977). Depending upon local circumstances, the stratigraphic profiles can be simple, with a single layer of pondfield sediment, or complex, with multiple strata of pondfield sediment, sometimes deeply buried, interrupted by intervals of alluvial and colluvial deposition that likely represent system breakdowns (Allen 1987; Yen et al. 1972).

Pondfields have proven difficult to date and firm estimates of when they were constructed are only rarely achieved. Early efforts tried to establish the chronology of pondfield use by dating unidentified pieces of charcoal collected from the pondfield sediments (e.g., Allen 1987; Allen et al. 2002; Yen et al. 1972). These efforts were unsuccessful because charcoal in the pondfield sediments has an uncertain, likely mixed, origin and cannot be confidently associated with use of the pondfield. Some of the charcoal might have derived in situ from burning the forest before the pondfields were constructed or from burning off weeds after a fallow period, but charcoal from points upstream also enters the pondfields with the irrigation water and is deposited in the pondfield sediments (Kirch 1977:255). The scope of the association problem is illustrated by the results from Trench 3 at Site G5-85 in Kāne'ohe on O'ahu, in which a stratigraphic sequence with four more or less distinct pondfield layers was dated fairly intensively (Allen 1987:78, 176). Dates range more than a thousand years within the same layer, include material that predates Polynesian discovery by centuries, and do not respect stratigraphic relations. These results clearly indicate the likely multiplicity of origins and the impossibility of confidently associating charcoal in the pondfield sediments with pondfield use.

Somewhat greater success has been achieved dating pondfield construction, instead of use. Here, it is easier to solve the problem of association, as shown by Spriggs and Kirch (1992:123), who dug a young piece of charcoal from alluvium underlying a pondfield soil exposed in a stream cut. Because the charcoal must be older than the pondfield soil above it, this dating evidence directly supports the claim that at least one of the pondfields in the upper Anahulu Valley was constructed following King Kamehameha I's conquest of O'ahu in 1804 (Spriggs and Kirch 1992). The strategy of isolating charcoal stratigraphically inferior to pondfields was later applied routinely with good results during excavations of several pondfield systems in Wailau, Moloka'i (McElroy 2007). Here excavations adjacent to pondfield bunds took care to collect charcoal and other datable materials from beneath a basal facing stone of the bund and identified short-lived materials for dating. McElroy argued that the charcoal "almost certainly represents burning for vegetation clearance before ... construction" (McElroy 2007:145) and this has sometimes been interpreted as if vegetation clearance immediately preceded construction, but all that can be said with confidence is that charcoal beneath the bund face is older than the pondfield construction event. The magnitude of the discrepancy cannot be estimated with any certainty given the evidence. The dates from the Wailau pondfield systems were calibrated absent the constraints of a stratigraphic model (McElroy 2007:140), and the resulting age estimates—for the growth of plants in the region prior to pondfield construction—have been interpreted as estimates of construction events (e.g., Kirch 2010a:145). This tactic potentially yields age estimates for pondfield construction that are too old because there is no guarantee that dated materials are not much older than the construction event. Bayesian calibration methods (Buck et al. 1996) make it possible to integrate the stratigraphic information yielded by the careful excavation procedure, which established the stratigraphic boundaries of two periods, one under the bund face that predates pondfield construction and another above the basal stones of the bund that postdates construction. Calibration of the oldest dated sample from Wailau, recovered beneath the bund of pondfield E-23 in the Lower Eliali'i pondfield system, indicates that the 95 percent highest posterior density region for the pondfield construction event is A.D. 1230–1809. Here, the imprecision of the construction date estimate, which extends into the historic period, is due to the lack of a terminus ante quem for pondfield construction. Finding material with which to establish a terminus ante quem is a difficult problem, but one that might be profitably addressed by future pondfield excavations. Because the calibration was carried out in a Bayesian framework, it is possible to evaluate as unlikely a recent hypothesis that "significant irrigation works were under construction in this large windward valley by AD 1200 to 1300" (Kirch 2010a:145). Given the dating model and the evidence, analysis with the BCal software package (Buck et al. 1999) shows this hypothesis has a 17 percent probability of being true.

Sweet Potato Gardens

Sweet potato was a late introduction to Hawai'i, and it arrived without the long history of horticultural experimentation and experience that accompanied the other crop plants. But the plant underwent a remarkable radiation in its time in Hawai'i, so that by the early twentieth century some 230 named varieties were known (Handy 1940:32–34), distinguished by the color and shape of their leaves, and the color of the leaf veins and the tubers. Yields of sweet potato were lower and labor inputs typically higher than with irrigated taro agriculture, mostly because sweet potatoes were grown in areas where considerable mulching was required. The plant thrived, however, in areas where the other crop plants grew with more difficulty and the development of rain-fed agricultural fields appears tied to the plant's introduction and establishment.

Archaeological investigation of rain-fed agricultural fields is dominated by the work of the Hawai'i Biocomplexity Project in the Leeward Kohala field system (Kirch, ed. 2010). The Leeward Kohala field system is compared here with the Kona field system, which has been investigated less thoroughly. The two systems are both characterized by well-developed agricultural facilities whose scale captures the imagination and fully justifies their characterization as field systems, but the two systems appear to have developed in different ways. Investigations of rain-fed agricultural fields outside of these two systems include studies on O'ahu (Allen 1987:94ff. Allen et al. 2002; Hommon 1970), the Kalaupapa Peninsula of Moloka'i (McCoy 2005), Kahikinui and Kaupo on Maui (Kirch 2010b), the Waimea field system (Burtchard and Tomonari-Tuggle 2004), and planting areas in pockets of old lava in South Kona (Allen and McAnany 1994) on Hawai'i Island, and small fields adjacent to temples on leeward Lāna'i Island (Dixon and Major 2011).

The Leeward Kohala field system refers to an extensive series of agricultural field walls that run perpendicular to the slope and, crosscutting them, curbstone-lined trails that ran through the field systems on their way to the coast. Facilities of this type cover an area of about 60 km^2 (Ladefoged et al. 2010:89) and include more than 570 km of walls and 190 km of trails (Ladefoged et al. 2010:93). Interspersed among the fields are numerous other structures interpreted as house foundations, temples, animal pens, and local agricultural features. The agricultural field walls are typically low constructions of rock and soil that would have broken the surface flow of the famous Kohala winds and served as platforms to plant windbreak crops such as sugarcane (Ladefoged et al. 2010:93), two measures that would have preserved moisture by reducing evapo-transpiration. In addition, the walls would have acted to control erosion by retarding downslope movement of agricultural soil.

Beneath the surface expression of the Leeward Kohala field system is an extensive horizon of agricultural soils that "show clear signs of clearing or cultivation, such as digging stick holes, churned sediments, and charcoal lenses or flecking" (Ladefoged and Graves 2008:778). The discovery of a probable sweet potato tuber in this pre-field system horizon (Ladefoged et al. 2005) indicates that this early stage of agriculture likely centered on the sweet potato, but other than this, little has been reported and the nature and extent of pre-field system agriculture are not clear.

The relative chronology of the field system features can be worked out in detail because the fabric-like structure of the field system—trails that connect the field system to the coast provide the warp for the weft of agricultural walls that divide fields from one another—yields an opportunity to establish relative ages of features at every intersection of a wall with a trail (see Kirch 1984:Figure 60). The stratigraphic relations of walls and trails has been studied in detail in a portion of the Leeward Kohala field system and several relative chronological interpretations have been proposed (Dye 2011b; Ladefoged et al. 2003; Ladefoged and Graves 2008). Using a graph-theoretic approach, Dye (2011b) was able to isolate three phases of wall construction divided by two periods of trail development. In each new phase of wall building, walls were typically shorter than in the previous phase and they served to divide the system into ever smaller fields. Construction effort appears to have increased over time based on the total length of walls built during each phase (Ladefoged and Graves 2000, 2008; Ladefoged et al. 2003).

Within the mesh of chronologically ordered construction events in the detailed study area, Ladefoged and Graves (2008) have carried out a sophisticated dating program that excavated beneath agricultural walls and under curbstones of trails to identify termini post quem for wall and curb construction events (Figure 4.4). The detailed dating record they have produced offers analytic opportunities unmatched in Hawaiian archaeology. Most of the ^{14}C age determinations are relatively young. Age determinations under

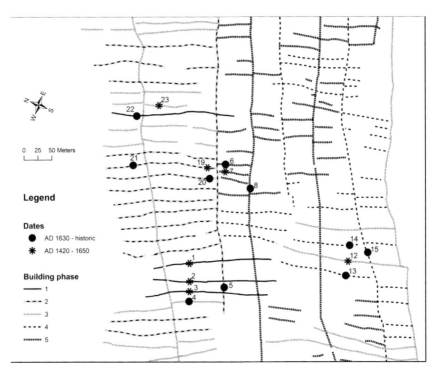

Figure 4.4: Map of the Leeward Kohala field system detailed study area.
Source: Ladefoged and Graves (2008). Reprinted with the kind permission
of T. Ladefoged.

walls built during the earliest phase of construction are less than 300
[14]C years old, and the youngest of these dates to 200 ± 40 B.P. The sample
collected from beneath a curbstone of the oldest trail dates to 130 ± 30 B.P.
Keeping in mind that these ^{14}C age determinations predate feature construction and that the field system was abandoned "within a few decades following European contact" (Kirch 2010a:153), most of the agricultural facilities
in the detailed study area were built within the span of about 100 ^{14}C years.

This rich set of data was analyzed by Dye (2011b) using Bayesian methods (Buck et al. 1996), which build a detailed chronological model of field
system development from the stratigraphic relations of the agricultural walls
and trails, and then fix this model in time with the ^{14}C age determinations.
The combination of young ^{14}C age determinations and the five-phase
chronological model yields dating results that are more precise than typically
achieved in Hawai'i. Given these data and the stratigraphic model, construction of agricultural facilities likely began late in the seventeenth century,

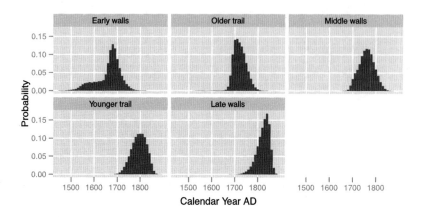

Figure 4.5: Chronology of facility construction in the
Leeward Kohala field system. Source: Dye (2011b).

with the tempo of construction increasing in the eighteenth century and
possibly reaching a peak in the historic period, after Cook's visit to the island
in 1779 (Figure 4.5).

The Kona field system has been investigated less intensively than the Leeward Kohala field system. The major investigations include a survey and
excavations performed in a proposed highway right-of-way (Schilt 1984), a
path-breaking set of excavations in a small portion of the field system now
used as an ethnobotanical garden (Allen 2001, ed.), and a more extensive
survey and excavation of field system features along the Keauhou coast
(Burtchard 1996; Burtchard et al. 1996) and above Kealakekua Bay
(Tomonari-Tuggle 2006). Other CRM investigations within the field system
are summarized by Allen (2001, ed., 2004).

The agricultural facilities of the Kona field system rival those of the Leeward Kohala field system in size and complexity, but they appear to have
been designed to solve different agronomic challenges and so take on a different form. The primary surface features of the field system, at least to the
modern observer, are long, low rocky mounds called *kuaiwi* that run with
the slope. Pairs of *kuaiwi* delineate narrow exposures of soil typically
divided by low lateral walls reminiscent of the walls in the Leeward Kohala
field system. The seaward margin of the Kona field system extends nearly to
the shore in many places, where it is easily accessible from coastal villages.
Consequently, at least in some parts of the Kona field system, most of the

structures appear to be related directly to agricultural uses, with relatively few auxiliary habitation and religious structures interspersed (Tomonari-Tuggle 2006:169).

Excavations in the Kona field system have exposed a stratum of modified sediment that runs beneath the field system facilities. The character of this layer varies from place to place but it is recognized in all areas of the field system that have been excavated. Allen was able to define "activity areas" characterized by pits, hearths, and remnant pavements and concentrations of charcoal and artifacts likely to have been used in agricultural fieldwork, such as sharp-edged volcanic glass flakes, small adzes, and abraders (Allen 2001:138–139). In other places, charcoal flecking, the occasional artifact, and construction of check dams and terracing indicate a pre-facility use of the area for activities "probably related to gardening" (Tomonari-Tuggle 2006:119).

Soils through most of the Kona field system are thin and their distribution is patchy. Outcrops of bare lava are common in the agricultural fields. The cultivator's response to this situation was to construct low walls to trap and retain sediment. These walls are the lateral walls seen today and also the subsurface expression of many *kuaiwi*, whose low, mounded caps are underlain by retaining walls whose stones are sometimes set upright (Tomonari-Tuggle 2006). The patches of agricultural soil bounded by these walls were typically prepared for cultivation by applying a green mulch and working it into the soil in the dry season. Planting of sweet potato was timed to coincide with the advent of the rainy season, after the mulch had composted in place. Horrocks and Rechtman (2009) suggest that sweet potato was the only tuberous crop grown in the Kona Field system, based on a study of plant microfossils that identified sweet potato and banana as the dominant crops.

The *kuaiwi* are rocky caps added to the tops of pre-existing walls. They likely had multiple functions as boundaries, as rock mulch, and as support for vine crops that do poorly when allowed to rest directly on the ground (Allen 2001, 2004). Often the *kuaiwi* materials were deposited directly on agricultural soils, but Tomonari-Tuggle (2006) found several instances where *kuaiwi* were constructed on more recent sediment deposits, reinforcing the evidence from earlier excavations that *kuaiwi* were a late feature on the landscape.

Early attempts to date activities in the Kona field system were carried out on unidentified wood charcoal with no control for the possible effects of old wood. Chronologies based on these materials are likely to be too old. Tomonari-Tuggle (2006) dated identified short-lived taxa and predictably found evidence for a younger chronology. The three-phase sequence posits a period of early gardening beginning A.D. 1500–1650, followed by a century from A.D. 1650 to 1750 when walled gardens consisting of lateral walls and the foundational precursors of the *kuaiwi* were constructed, followed sometime after A.D. 1750 by construction of the *kuaiwi* features characteristic of the Kona field system (Tomonari-Tuggle 2006:126).

The degree to which field system development was a bottom-up process initiated by cultivators working in a more or less coordinated fashion or a top-down process initiated and coordinated by elites is an open question. Allen (2004) has argued that the early part of the sequence was characterized by the efforts of cultivators to minimize risk, and that efforts initiated by elites to intensify production were not evident until near the end of the sequence. The evidence cited for imposition of elite authority in field system development is the regional pattern of *kuaiwi* construction, and in particular, the great length of *kuaiwi* (Allen 2004), such that they typically span many individual agricultural fields. Given the dating evidence set out by Tomonari-Tuggle (2006), imposition of elite authority took place late in the eighteenth century. However, Tomonari-Tuggle (2006) has noted that *kuaiwi* are in fact discontinuous and that temporary habitation features are often found built into the ends of *kuaiwi* at these discontinuities. Her characterization of field system development, including *kuaiwi* construction, as "an organic evolution formed by immediate environmental and topographic conditions" (Tomonari-Tuggle 2006:160) supports the idea that the Kona field system was a bottom-up development throughout its history. Thus, to the extent that elite authority structured development of the Kona field system, if at all, it appears to have been confined to the late eighteenth century.

Animals, Wild and Domesticated

In contrast to the recent theoretical interest in the development of agricultural facilities, the ways Hawaiians raised and captured their animal foods are relatively neglected in the archaeological literature. Animal husbandry was highly developed, especially the rearing of pigs, which were offered in great numbers at feasts and ceremonies. The materials for the theoretical exercise appear to be present. There is a rich ethnographic literature on Hawaiian fishing practices that documents a mastery of the sea and an ability to take any kind of reef fish, a wide variety of pelagic fishes, and bottom fish to depths of 200 fathoms (e.g., Kaha'ulelio 2006; Titcomb 1972; Maly and Maly 2003). Inshore waters to the edge of the reef or within a mile of shore where reefs are absent were considered part of the *ahupua'a*, their use restricted to residents and regulated to some degree by local chiefs (Kosaki 1954). Fishing seasons for the pelagic fishes mackerel scad and skipjack tuna were opened by rituals carried out on behalf of the high chiefs (Malo 1951:189, 208). The technology needed to develop fishponds capable of producing more than a million kilograms of fish annually was invented locally and deployed in a variety of environments with a highly developed engineering skill.

Fishponds

Hawaiians invented a highly productive system of aquaculture that was deployed on a broad scale across the archipelago (Kikuchi 1976; Wyban 1992). Fishponds were constructed in a variety of environments in sizes that ranged from less than a hectare to more than 200 ha. Some of the fishponds were temporary productions. Fallow taro pondfields were stocked with freshwater gobies that could be raised and harvested until the field was put back into taro production. Other fishponds were more or less permanent fixtures of the landscape. Low marshy areas near streams or at the back beach were augmented by modifying water sources and installing sluice grates, a clever device whose closely spaced vertical bars permitted the free flow of water and small fish, but which trapped larger fish within the pond. The apogee of fishpond construction was the large coastal ponds constructed in sheltered waters mostly on the lee sides of islands (Figure 4.6). The long stone walls of these ponds, with one or more sluice grates, are prominent features of the modern landscape, though many of the ponds known from historical records (e.g., Cobb 1903), in particular those of the south coast of O'ahu around Honolulu, are now buried by coastal development. In areas where the abandoned fishponds are not buried there is some interest in restoring them to productivity (e.g., Wyban 1992). Farber (1997) advocates a community-based planning approach to restore numerous fishponds on the south coast of Moloka'i Island, and also identifies the significant regulatory obstacles faced by that effort.

The fishpond technology developed in ancient Hawai'i was an effective food producer. At the height of production, the 360 coastal fishponds for

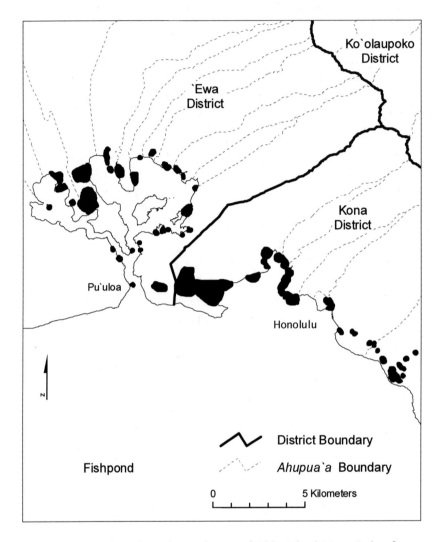

Figure 4.6: Fishponds on the south coast of O'ahu Island. Note: Only a few
of the ponds are extant; most of them were filled in the late nineteenth
and early twentieth centuries.

which data are available are estimated to have yielded about a million kilograms of fish a year (Kikuchi 1976), a figure that discounts the undoubtedly
substantial production of the more numerous inland ponds. A key to these
yields, regardless of pond location, was a calm, shallow-water environment
to which nutrient-rich freshwater was continually introduced. The pond

water was shallow, so sunlight could penetrate to the bottom, where rich benthic flora and fauna were food for the herbivorous fish that were the prized product of the ponds, principally the mullet and the milkfish. The benthos created by the pondfields is analogous to grass, and the fish graze it like sheep or cattle in a terrestrial pasture.

It is something of a paradox that an achievement as great as the invention of the traditional aquacultural system, engineered to be productive in a wide variety of environments, is mostly ignored by Hawaiian tradition. When Samuel Kamakau chronicled the works of the people of old in the mid-nineteenth century, he could only infer that the "making of the fishponds and their walls is very ancient" (Kamakau 1976:47), presumably because he could not associate the fishponds with the genealogical framework of Hawaiian tradition. In contrast to the temples, another monumental construction of old Hawai'i whose connection to individual elites is often recorded by tradition, names of fishpond builders appear to be lost in time. When traditions do indicate fishpond builders, the reference is typically to the *Menehune*, a legendary race of small people with remarkable development skills. Today, the best hope for recovering this history of fishpond development is archaeology.

Unfortunately, the fishponds have proved difficult to date with archaeological methods. The problems are conceptually similar to the problems of dating irrigated pondfields, discussed earlier; organic materials in fishpond sediments derived from multiple sources, so their association with pond construction and use is problematic. The difficulty is heightened by the uncertainty in distinguishing fishpond deposits from other natural deposits. This is especially the case in the fishponds established in natural ponds, such as those commonly found in the back beach. Here, the naturally calm, shallow-water conditions would have supported benthic flora and fauna indistinguishable from a fishpond. Another source of uncertainty in the coastal ponds is the mix of marine and terrestrial organic material. This mixing is evident in the $\delta^{13}C$ values from coastal fishpond sediments, which are intermediate between terrestrial values around −25 per mill and marine values around 0 per mill. Unless the proportion of organic material from each source is known, it is not possible to make precise corrections for the apparent age of marine organic material. An attempt to date the development of fishponds at Pearl Harbor by one of us (TSD) underestimated the problems of association and recognition, which were exacerbated by the use of paleoenvironmental coring equipment to work through the thick applications of fill material at most of the ponds (Athens 2000). The results of this project and another attempt to date materials collected from fishpond sediments at a buried pond near Honolulu (McGerty et al. 1997) are sufficiently variable to indicate the operation of association and recognition problems and should be discounted.

A potentially more productive approach to dating fishponds was partially worked out some years earlier during an archaeological reconnaissance survey of an Army fort in Waikīkī. Trenches excavated with a backhoe, and positioned with the aid of a nineteenth-century map of fishponds and ditches, exposed aquacultural features long since buried by development of tourist facilities in Waikīkī, including the earthen wall of Loko Paweo fishpond and the large irrigation ditch that ran beside the fishpond (Davis 1989:45). Organic materials for dating were collected from sediments below the ditch and within the earthen wall of the ditch, two contexts with materials that predate construction and use of the ditch and presumably the fishpond, as well. Davis interpreted the dates in the ad hoc manner typical of the day, but a Bayesian calibration that includes the stratigraphic information indicates that the wall between the fishpond and the ditch was constructed sometime after the mid-fifteenth century.

Distribution of Animal Remains

Vertebrate and invertebrate faunal remains are routinely recovered during archaeological excavations, identified, and reported. The theoretical framework for this effort was set out by Kirch (1982a), who compared and contrasted faunal assemblages from three coastal sites. The ecological framework developed by Kirch is more widely applicable, and it is used here to compare diverse faunal assemblages ranging from the coast to the summit region of Mauna Kea. The comparison is carried out at a general level designed to illustrate broad patterns in the distribution of animal remains.

The 23 sites used in the faunal analysis are located on the leeward side of Hawai'i Island in the districts of Kona and Kohala (Figure 4.7). Fifteen of the sites are located on the coast, which in this region is dry and characterized by recent lava flows (Table 4.2). Agriculture was out of the question along most of the coast and the remains of fields are found at higher elevations where rainfall was more plentiful. Four of the sites are located within the agricultural

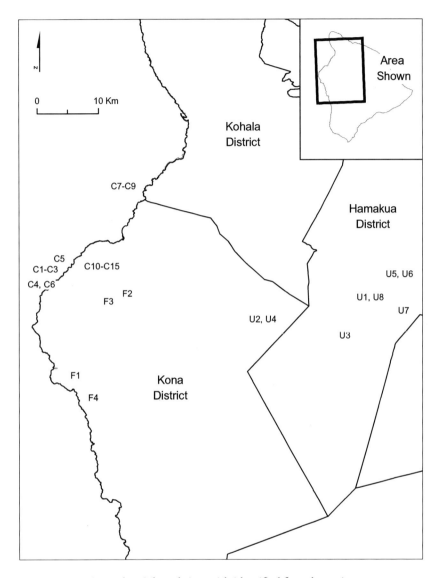

Figure 4.7: Selected sites with identified faunal remains.

field system, all of them in the south where arable soils are within relatively easy walking distance of the coast. The upland limits of agriculture are defined by soils depleted of nutrients through too much rainfall (Vitousek et al. 2004). Above this line are the uplands, which were resources for the bird feathers used in elite regalia, nesting colonies of seabirds for food, wood for

Table 4.2: Sites with Identified Faunal Remains.

Site	Label	Setting	Reference
Coastal			
50–10–18–5341	C1	Open	Dye (2002:28ff.)
50–10–18–5349	C2	Lava tube	Dye (2002:32ff.)
50–10–18–5354	C3	Lava tube	Dye (2002:34ff.)
T-140, fea. B	C4	Lava tube	Dye et al. (2002:232)
50–10–18–23355	C5	Lava tube	Dye et al. (2002:232)
T-164, fea. A	C6	Lava tube	Dye et al. (2002:232)
50–10–10–11239	C7	Blister cave	Jensen (1990:Table A-5)
50–10–10–11243	C8	Cave	Jensen (1990:Table A-5)
50–10–10–11244	C9	Cave	Jensen (1990:Table A-5)
50–10–19–16047	C10	Overhang	Goodfellow et al. (1992:Table 19)
50–10–19–16048	C11	Open	Goodfellow et al. (1992:Table 19) F
50–10–19–16061	C12	Open	Goodfellow et al. (1992:Table 19)
50–10–19–16063	C13	Open/overhang	Goodfellow et al. (1992:Table 19)
50–10–19–16069	C14	Open	Goodfellow et al. (1992:Table 19)
50–10–19–16185	C15	Caves/overhang	Goodfellow et al. (1992:Table 19)
Fields			
50–10–37–5151	F1	Cave	Schilt (1984:79–89)
50–10–28–17931	F2	Lava tube	Goodfellow and Head (1995)
50–10–28–17938	F3	Lava tube	Goodfellow and Head (1995)
50–10–37–5157	F4	Cave	Schilt (1984:89–98)
Upland			
50–10–22–16238	U1	Cave	McCoy (1986)
50–10–31–19495	U2	Lava tube	Reinman and Pantaleo (1998:60–62)
50–10–31–19490	U3	Lava tube	Reinman and Pantaleo (1998:43–51)
50–10–31–19497	U4	Lava tube	Reinman and Pantaleo (1998:66–68)
Ko'oko'olau no. 1	U5	Rockshelter	McCoy (1990:104–107)
'U'au	U6	Rockshelter	McCoy (1990:104–107)
Waikahalulu	U7	Rockshelter	McCoy (1990:104–107)
Hopukani no. 1	U8	Rockshelter	McCoy (1990:104–107)

canoes and construction, and high-quality tool basalt for adzes. Eight of the sites are from this upland region on the slopes of Mauna Kea. Six of the upland sites are located downslope of the end moraines of the glaciers that once covered the mountaintop. The other two rockshelter sites, Ko'oko'olau no. 1 and 'U'au, are nearer the summit within a formerly glaciated area where tabular blocks of the best quality adze rock are found. These shelters, located well above the tree line, are part of the Mauna Kea adze quarry and are associated with large mounds of adze-making debitage.

The faunal remains recovered from the sites are classified according to zoological class, with the exception that rats are broken out from the mam-

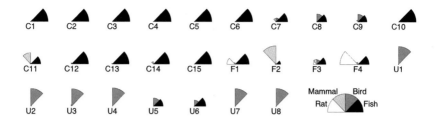

Figure 4.8: Faunal assemblages from Leeward Hawai'i sites.
Note: see Table 4.2 for information on the sites represented.

mal class (Figure 4.8). Rats are treated specially because, unlike pigs and dogs, there is no traditional evidence that rats were eaten in Hawai'i (but see Kirch and O'Day 2003). The class of birds potentially includes domestic chickens as well as various seabirds, but in all cases chickens are rare or absent in the recovered remains and seabird bones predominate. The remains classified as fish are predominantly bony fishes, but elements from cartilagenous fishes are also present, primarily shark teeth.

The figure indicates regional differences in the archaeological faunal assemblages. Coastal assemblages are dominated by fish; assemblages from sites in the agricultural field system are the most diverse, with prominent mammal and rat components, while the upland sites are characterized by birds. There is, of course, considerable variability within each region, and this variability is brought out in the following sections.

Coastal Sites

Kirch (1982a) was a strong early proponent of the identification and analysis of faunal remains from Hawaiian archaeological sites. He identified a close relationship between marine faunal assemblages from coastal sites and the fauna present in the immediate coastal environment that has been verified by subsequent analyses. Literally hundreds of CRM reports indicate that the kinds of shellfish recovered from the sites are found immediately offshore, where ethnographic materials indicate that they were likely collected by women and children (Titcomb 1978:327) who did not collect indiscriminately, but instead targeted more desirable taxa (Jones and Kirch 2007). Kirch also identified the preponderance of inshore and benthic fish in the assemblages, with only rare pelagic taxa, another pattern that has been verified by subsequent analyses (Chiu 2004; Collins 1995; Gordon 1993; Goto 1986; Kirch et al. 2003; O'Leary 2005). The correspondence between the excavated fishbone assemblages and census data for fishes in the marine environment is marked, indicating an ability to take all kinds of fish and a broad range of suitable food fish (Dye et al. 2002:285).

Most fish appear to have been taken by angling, netting, and spearing, with the precise mix of fishing strategies determined by the offshore environment and the degree to which reefs are developed. Angling and bottom fishing appear to have been more important at places that lack developed reefs (Kirch 1982a; cf. Goto 1986). O'Leary (2005) reports evidence for an increase in angling at the reef edge over time. The fish identified in the archaeological collections are typically small- to medium-size individuals (Kirch et al. 2010:156; O'Day 2001:294).

Surprisingly, fish raised in fishponds are rarely identified in the archaeological collections. Although it is tempting to posit cultural factors that might have determined which fish made it into the deposits and which did not, identification biases might also be at work (Hartzell 1997:254). Weisler (1993) pointed out the importance of otoliths, distinctive ear stones typically overlooked in faunal analyses, for identifying the full range of taxa present in archaeological deposits. The potential magnitude of this effect was illustrated recently with the recovery and identification of 260 bonefish otoliths at a coastal site on Oʻahu (McElroy et al. 2006:154). Identification of the fish otoliths radically changed the rank order of fish in the identified assemblage. Previously, bonefish were thought to be rarely captured because only a single bone had been identified from extensive excavations in the region. The otolith identifications indicate that bonefish were among the most common fish in the catch.

Kirch (1982a:465, Figure 2) also noted the preponderance of fish remains at the coastal sites, with a terrestrial component that varied according to the proximity of settlements and agricultural facilities. The coastal Kawailoa site on Oʻahu, a habitation site located near agricultural fields, yielded a diverse faunal assemblage with relatively large numbers of pig, dog, and rat bones (Collins 1995). The coastal sites in Figure 4.8 are all distant from inland agricultural fields and most of them show the expected predominance of fish. Many of the sites yielded a few mammal bones that likely represent raw material for fishhook manufacture, rather than the remains of food consumed at the site. A possible exception is an open site (C11) with a complex history that was used for human burial. The other exceptions are three sites (C7, C8, and C9) at the northern end of the sample that include a relatively large seabird bone component. It is likely that the seabirds were captured at artificial nesting sites, so-called *pāhoehoe* pits, prepared by bashing holes in suitable lava flows. One seabird species, the dark-rumped petrel, nests in similar pits at higher elevations today (Moniz 1997; Moniz-Nakamura et al. 1998). The presence of seabirds in the pits near the coast is signaled by pieces of pumice that geochemical analysis indicates originated from the arc of volcanoes that stretches from Japan to Alaska (Dye 2002). Although rafts of pumice are relatively common in the Pacific, the pieces recovered from the pits were too small to have floated to Hawai'i. However, Japan and Alaska are within the foraging range of seabirds that nest in Hawai'i. Several of the pumice pieces from the coastal pits were chemically weathered, and a geochemical analysis of the weathered surface showed elevated levels of phosphorous consistent with residence in the gut of a seabird. One function of the *pāhoehoe* pits, which are numerous along the leeward Hawai'i Island coast, appears to have been to provide a potential nesting ground for seabirds.

Sites in the Agricultural Field System

In contrast to the coastal sites with their heavy reliance on fish, sites in areas with arable soil typically yield a more diverse faunal assemblage in which pigs and dogs play a prominent role in addition to fish. This diverse assemblage is exemplified by site F2 (Figure 4.8), a cave with good preservation, but diverse assemblages are also found at open sites (e.g., Hartzell 1997; Kirch and O'Day 2003). These agricultural field system sites contain shellfish and fish remains similar to coastal sites nearby, indicating regular transport of food inland from the coast.

The uneven distribution of pig and dog bone evident in Figure 4.8 is not solely a feature of site location. Sites with larger architectural features tend to yield a larger proportion of pig and dog bone. This pattern has been interpreted in different ways: Dixon et al. (2002) distinguish between permanent house sites and field shelters, while Kirch and O'Day (2003) distinguish between larger features used by elites and smaller features used by commoners. Pig bone is more ubiquitous than dog bone, and when the two co-occur, pig bones typically outnumber dog bones by a substantial margin (see Kirch and O'Day 2003). Investigations of age at death of pigs and dogs indicate that immature and juvenile pigs were most often eaten, but that larger percentages of dogs were eaten when mature (Kirch and Collins 1989:65; Kirch and Sahlins 1992:41; Kirch et al. 2010:157; O'Day 2001:295).

Sites within the agricultural field system sometimes yield large quantities of rat bones (Figure 4.8, F4). This situation has led to the speculation that rats were eaten. The evidence for this is that rat bones are present in the assemblages in a condition that is "fragmentary, burned and covered in carbonized material" (Kirch and O'Day 2003:491; cf. Kirch et al. 2010:157). However, the further speculation that "elites were not consuming them, perhaps as a show of status or taste" (Kirch and O'Day 2003:491) appears to be confounded by the presence of rat bones in the purportedly elite sites.

High Elevation Forest and Alpine Sites

Inland of the agricultural field system, at sites in the high-elevation forest, the nature of the faunal assemblages changes radically. The diverse faunal assemblages at sites in the agricultural field system give way to sites where the assemblages are dominated by bird bone to the virtual exclusion of other kinds of bone (Figure 4.8, U1–U4, U7, U8). These sites lack shellfish remains and appear to be unusual in the absence of coastal food remains. Most of the bird bone from the sites has been identified as either petrel or goose. These birds were likely captured from nesting sites, some of which were likely *pāhoehoe* pits similar to those near the coast described earlier (Moniz-Nakamura et al. 1998). The petrels and geese were cooked with the aid of ritually charged cook stones whose wide distribution at sites in the high forest suggests that they were kept in the shelter caves between visits (P. McCoy 2011). The presence of small numbers of songbird bones led to the suggestion that sites in the high forest were used by bird hunters who captured and consumed petrels and geese while they were gathering bright colored songbird feathers used to manufacture elite regalia (Athens et al. 1991). However, songbirds are not confined to faunal assemblages from the high forest, where bird catchers were traditionally active, but are found in assemblages from the coast to the top of Mauna Kea (Collins 1995; McCoy 1990:106).

Higher on the mountain at rockshelter sites within the Mauna Kea Adze Quarry, the faunal assemblages include marine resources along with birds (Figure 4.8). Here, shellfish remains were recovered in small quantities, but fish bones were abundant. The list of fish identified at the rockshelters includes several taxa that were taken either by trolling or bottom-fishing from a canoe. Also present are gobies, which are freshwater fish likely taken from a stream on the trip up the mountain (McCoy 1990:105). This mix of fish taxa contrasts with faunal assemblages from the leeward coast, where inshore reef fish are present almost exclusively and there are no permanent streams. Perhaps the faunal assemblages indicate that inhabitants of the rockshelters came from the windward side of the island where streams flow year-round and fishermen typically work from canoes because reefs along the windward coast are poorly developed.

Conclusions

The landscapes transported to Hawai'i by Polynesians supported a large and healthy population. Archaeologists have made much progress in understanding the process of their establishment, although many questions remain. On present evidence, the settlement period between discovery and establishment of an archaeologically recognizable human population appears to have lasted well over a century. It is tempting to interpret this gap in the archaeological record as a sampling issue, but enough archaeological work has been done to justify entertaining the idea that the settlement process was multi-generational, rather than an event or a process carried out within the lifetime of an individual. It would be a mistake to underestimate the difficulty of the settlement enterprise, which routinely required months-long ocean voyages through the uncertainties of the doldrums. Perhaps the first century or so after the islands were discovered was characterized by a small, transient population that split time between Hawai'i and the homeland.

Paleoenvironmental investigations leave little doubt that introduction of the Polynesian rat early in the process brought about major environmental change. The stout *Pritchardia* palms that characterized the primeval lowland forest could not withstand predation by rats on their seeds and they were replaced by shrubs and herbs, effectively "softening" the forest for its subsequent clearing for agricultural use. Useful plants, such as the candlenut tree, established viable populations at this time, conceivably without active tending by a resident population.

The histories of the South American plants sweet potato and bottle gourd indicate that the transported landscapes established in Hawai'i responded to changes in the homeland over a period of at least a century and perhaps more. The sample size of dated Polynesian introductions is still small and it is likely that more work along these lines will substantially revise the current picture.

Archaeologists have been somewhat less successful documenting the histories of food-producing practices and facilities. The fishponds and taro pondfields that are so prominent on the landscape are difficult to date because the organic matter found within them cannot be confidently associated with construction or use of the facility. A more promising approach, which dates material from contexts stratigraphically inferior to the facilities, has seen limited application. Future work along these lines is likely to make substantial changes to our understanding of when these facilities were built.

Dating efforts in the rain-fed agricultural fields have yielded more satisfying results. They appear to show that the facilities characteristic of intensification were constructed late in the precontact period and into the historic period. The early history of these field systems is preserved in a deposit beneath the more recent field system features. The nature and extent of this pre-facility deposit is poorly known and future research is vital.

5

Technology and Craft Economy

Contact-period Hawaiians practiced and elaborated labor-intensive technologies and craft economies that were commensurate with the cultural and economic imperatives of their island society. Like other Polynesian societies, Hawaiians crafted materials to extract and produce their food, construct their houses, and assert their gender, social status, and political power. Materials that were suitable for traditional technologies are abundant in Hawaii's islands and include basalt, wood, plant fibers, shell, human and non-human bone, coral, and feathers (Abbott 1992; Buck 1957; Starzecka 1975).

Hawaiian artisans during the post-contact period used such materials to craft products including stone adzes; fishing gear such as hooks, lures, and nets; canoes; weapons; wood bowls; cordage; and barkcloth clothing, such as loin cloths and skirts. Other goods included plant-fiber mats, baskets, and rain capes; games and musical instruments; and feather standards, cloaks, crown-like helmets, and other regalia for Hawaiian elites. Many of these items were witnessed and collected by the first Europeans to visit Hawaiʻi, including Captain Cook, and their roles in contact-period society were recorded by native historians (e.g., Malo 1951) who retained knowledge of their cultural meanings and technologies of manufacture. Museum ethnographic collections from the contact period offer a more or less synchronic perspective on Hawaiian craft economies in the post-contact period (e.g., Buck 1957, 1943, 1944; Brigham 1899, 1902, 1906a, 1906b, 1911; Dalton 1897; Dickey 1928; Dodge 1939; Kaeppler 1978; Stokes 1906, 1928; Summers 1999, 1989). Studies of material culture have offered valuable insights on the technology and political economy of their use and meaning in contact-period society. However, questions about the long-term historical development of Hawaiian technologies and craft economies require scholars to consult the archaeological record (e.g., Allen 1996; Pfeffer 2001).

Table 5.1: Gendered Labor for Selected Hawaiian Crafts Described in
Selected Ethnohistoric Sources.

Artisan	Featherwork	Cordage	Tapa	Mats	Canoes	Fishhooks	Stone adzes
Female adult	X	X	X	X	-	-	-
Male adult	X	X	-	-	X	X	X
Female sub-adult	-	X	-	-	-	-	-
Male sub-adult	-	X	?		?	?	?

As we noted earlier in Chapter 1, archaeologists who examine Hawaiian technology and craft economies often apply the direct historical approach to interpret traditional organization of labor, and accounts by Europeans and native historians who lived in the late eighteenth century and early nineteenth century figure prominently. Simply put, contact-period Hawaiians adhered to a traditional *kapu* (taboo) institution wherein labor (in the ideal, at least) was gendered: agriculture and fishing, for example, was practiced by males, as were certain craft activities, such as the manufacture of canoes (Table 5.1). Women, in contrast, devoted much of their labor to the production of plant fiber mats and other crafts, such as featherwork (Linnekin 1990, 1988). Contact-period Hawaiian crafting was hereditary and individuals acquired their skills from household elders (Lass 1998:20).

Perhaps more importantly, crafting in contact-period Hawaiian society was a divinely ascribed undertaking, and there were recognized "specialists" for most classes of products (Malo 1951:79; see Lass 1998:26). Moreover, family gods throughout Polynesia were associated with particular crafts and occupations, and individuals worshipped the particular deity that presided over her/his occupation (Malo 1951:81; see Lass 1998:21).

Certain crafts were practiced under chiefly oversight and sponsorship during the post-contact period, such as featherwork and war-canoe construction. Other products, such as barkcloth and mats, were potentially made by part-time specialists who were women and were accepted by chiefs as tribute or taxation (Lass 1998:26). This historically documented pattern in craft specialization underlies a long-standing question in Hawaiian archaeology: Were some goods made by independent or attached specialists (Brumfiel and Earle 1987) in ancient Hawai'i? A complementary debate centers on the following question: Did Hawaiian craft goods circulate through exchange among individuals or groups of people who resided in different territories, or were such populations economically autonomous?

Because stone adzes are well preserved in the archaeological record, studies of their technology, production, and circulation have been fundamental to models of pre-contact craft economy in Hawai'i.

Stone Adze Technology and Economy

Archaeologists who study traditional Hawaiian craft economies before European contact have focused most of their energy on stone adzes, and only limited attention has been devoted to expedient flake cutting tools that were made with volcanic glass and used for plant fiber processing and butchering animal protein such as fish, pig, and dog (Athens et al. 1991; Barrera and Kirch 1973; Weisler 1990; Williams 2004:116). Stone adzes of varying sizes were used to carve wood into bowls, house posts, canoes, weapons, and sacred images of gods.

Archaeologists who work in Hawai'i and other areas in Polynesia have confirmed that its artisans practiced a similar adze production technology; they used bi-directional reduction of short, thick flakes to fabricate tools with quadrangular or trapezoidal cross sections (Cleghorn 1984; Weisler 1990:38–41). Adzes often have a contracting tang behind the shoulder to facilitate hafting. Moreover, their cutting edges were ground and polished before they were hafted on wood handles (Figure 5.1). The cutting edge of a Hawaiian adze blade is transverse to its hafting element. At quarries that lacked raw material suitable for producing short, thick flakes, such as small, rounded cobbles in stream beds, bi-directional flaking was ineffective (e.g., Bayman and Moniz-Nakamura 2001). Bi-directional flaking was instead most effective at Hawaiian quarries, such as Mauna Kea, with its outcrops of dense, fine-grained, tabular blocks of basalt (Figure 5.2).

Because stone adzes were vital in traditional society, and they are relatively abundant in the archaeological record, they offer an exceptional opportunity to interpret a pre-contact craft economy. Stone adzes were needed to clear forests for agricultural production, and to fashion the canoes used in offshore fishing, inter-island exchange, and warfare; and they directly linked the subsistence and political economies of traditional Hawaiian society (Lass 1994:68). In the early contact period, all of these activities—agriculture, marine exploitation, warfare, and inter-island exchange—lay within the administrative purview of Hawaiian chiefs. The value of labor that was invested heavily in stone adze production is signaled by non-production locales where they were

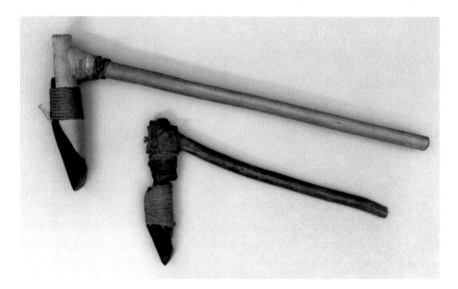

Figure 5.1: Hafted adzes. Top: adze, Bishop Museum catalog 3101. Bottom: swivel head adze, Bishop Museum catalog 3116. Photographed for University of Hawai'i Committee for the Preservation of Hawaiian Language, Art, and Culture. Reproduced courtesy of B. P. Bishop Museum.

Figure 5.2: Debitage pile at the Mauna Kea adze quarry. Note: The upright stones on the horizon are part of a shrine and stand approximately 50 cm high. Photograph by E. K. Komori.

re-worked and re-sharpened (e.g., Olszewski 2007); perhaps it was desirable to recycle stone adzes since they were energetically costly.

Traditional histories and contact-period accounts, in tandem with studies of the archaeological record, offer hypotheses concerning the fundamental importance of stone adzes in the political and economic dynamics of Hawaiian society. In the early post-contact period, the construction of war canoes—more than 1,000 in some instances—required large stone adzes like those that were manufactured at Mauna Kea, the largest quarry in Oceania. Great numbers of stone adzes would have been necessary for clearing forests for agricultural fields on newly conquered islands; adzes were probably used for tilling such fields, too (Dockall 2000). Of particular importance, a variety of stone adzes and chisels were necessary to sculpt material representations of gods and deities that were emplaced at the most important religious temples, such as *luakini*, for staging human sacrifice and other offerings to the gods (Valeri 1985a).

As we noted in Chapter 1, archaeologists such as Kenneth Emory (1968) and Yosihiko Sinoto (1968) studied Hawaiian stone adzes and other artifacts, such as fishhooks, to construct culture-historical chronologies. Emory's study of 265 adzes from Bishop Museum and other collections led him to conclude that the early Hawaiian adze kit was highly variable and that it included quadrangular, plano-convex, triangular, and reverse triangular cross sections, and that some early forms were tanged (Cleghorn 1992:130; Emory 1968:164). Moreover, only quadrangular adzes, most of them with tangs, persisted into later periods of the Hawaiian chronological sequence.

Patrick Kirch (1985:184) advanced the plausible argument that because late prehistoric Hawaiian adzes were seemingly standardized, they reflected the development of adze-making specialists, although he did not have the benefit of a well-dated assemblage of adzes (Cleghorn 1992:130). A detailed metric and non-metric study of 147 adzes from dated archaeological contexts at 21 sites on five islands confirmed that adze forms were variable throughout the Hawaiian chronological sequence, even though rectangular forms became increasingly common (Cleghorn 1992).

Although this finding does not preclude the rise of adze-making specialists, it does reveal that Hawaiian adzes were fabricated into a variety of forms that had different functions throughout the pre-contact period. As Cleghorn (1992:145) notes, large adzes might have been used for felling trees, whereas small adzes could have been used for fine carving. In either

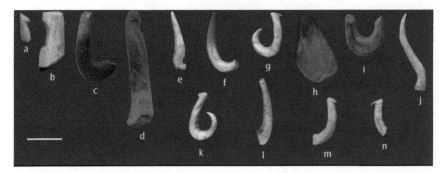

Figure 5.3: Bone fishhooks. a, c, d, f, g, i, k–n: one-piece hooks and hook fragments; b, h: unfinished hooks; e, j: two-piece hook points. Note: The scale bar is 1 cm. Source: McElroy et al. (2006).

case, like fishhooks, the use of adzes to assess the relative age of a Hawaiian archaeological site, or to construct a chronological sequence, fell out of favor with the rise of New Archaeology.

Early Fishhook Studies

The use of archaeology for the modern purpose of investigating change over time began in Hawai'i with the study of fishhooks. Excavations at 33 sites in the 1950s, along with inspection of private collections, yielded 4,159 fishhooks in a wide variety of forms made from human, bird, pig, and dog bone (Figure 5.3); dog teeth; and pearl (Figure 5.4) and turtle shell (Emory et al. 1968:3, 21). The hooks were classified formally into three types: one-piece, two-piece, and composite hooks. There were two types of composite hooks, one designed for the capture of bonito and the other for octopus. In both types, hooks were attached to a rig that included a lure. Two-piece hooks consist of a separate point or point-tip and shank and include a wide variety of forms generally designed to take larger fish. The one-piece hooks were divided into jabbing hooks, which the fisherman set with a tug on the line, and rotating hooks, which set themselves through the action of the fish striking the bait (Figure 5.5). Also recovered and described were tools for shaping, reshaping, and finishing the hooks, including "coral and lava saws and files, shell drill points, and coral balance wheels for the drills" (Emory et al. 1968:19). In addition to these tools, the fishhook-maker's toolkit is now thought to have included a variety of slate pencil urchin spine abraders

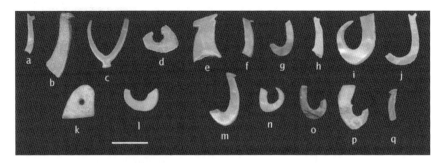

Figure 5.4: Pearl shell fishhook fragments and unfinished hooks.
Note: The scale bar is 1 cm. Source: McElroy et al. (2006).

(Calugay and McElroy 2005) and some very fine abraders fashioned from the diminutive spines of *Echinothrix diadema* (Figure 5.6).

Excavations at three sites near the southern end of Hawai'i Island were especially productive. Two of the sites, the Pu'u Ali'i site (H1) and the H8 site at Wai'ahukini, were stratified and excavation techniques were sufficient to preserve evidence for change over time in fishhook form. The lashing devices at the base of two-piece fishhook points and shanks showed a trend

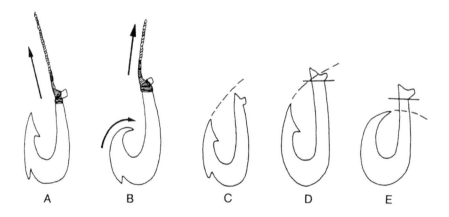

Figure 5.5: Jabbing and rotating hooks. a: the jabbing hook point is set with a pull;
b: the rotating hook point rotates with a pull; c: the extended point curve line does
not intersect the shank of a jabbing hook; d, e: the extended point curve line
intersects the shank of rotating hooks. Source: Sinoto (1991). Reproduced
with the kind permission of Y. H. Sinoto.

73

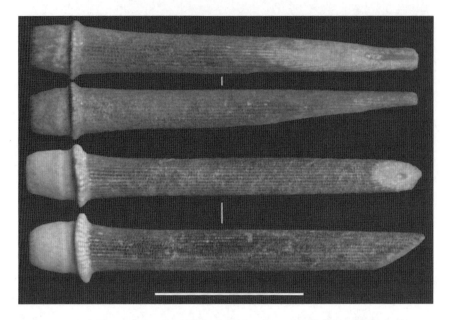

Figure 5.6: Two Diminutive *Echinothrix Diadema* abraders. Note: The scale bar is 1 cm. Source: McElroy et al. (2006).

from a base with a multiple-notched lashing device to one with a single notch and a knob at the end, particularly at the H8 site. Somewhat later, a detailed study of the lashing devices of one-piece hooks from the three Hawai'i Island sites and the Nualolo shelter site on Kaua'i showed an analogous change over time from notched to knobbed devices (Sinoto 1968). In both cases, the changes were identified and displayed stratigraphically, the results presented by layers and levels within sites. Green (1971) generalized these site-specific findings and showed that it was possible to seriate both the two-piece and one-piece hooks. However, he concluded that the seriations did not represent chronologies because the fishhook data were from archaeological units of disparate durations, a violation of one of the method's requirements (Dunnell 1970).

Most of the work on fishhooks since that time has focused on issues of classification or function, with an emphasis on distinguishing style and function in an evolutionary framework (Allen 1996; Graves and McElroy 2005; Pfeffer 2001; Sinoto 1991; Weisler and Walter 2002). This promising theoretical work has not spawned a tradition of fishhook studies in Hawaiian archaeology. Partly, this is due to the fact that many of the excavations from the 1950s, including the important Puʻu Aliʻi site, were never worked up for publication, so the details of stratigraphic distribution are incompletely known. Important exceptions to this generalization are the sites at Nualolo Kai on Kauaʻi, which were first excavated in the 1950s and have been subsequently re-studied (Graves et al. 2005; Hunt 2005), including a re-classification and description of the fishing gear and manufacturing tool kits (Calugay and McElroy 2005; Graves and McElroy 2005). More importantly, the excavations in the 1950s were some of the last ones to yield collections of fishhooks large enough to analyze in this way. Already in the 1950s, looting sites for their fishhooks was a problem (Emory et al. 1968:x–xi), which the territorial legislature's 1955 act to protect archaeological sites did not solve. By the 1980s, coastal cave sites with stratified deposits where fishhooks were typically plentiful had been thoroughly looted by collectors whose methods, including the use of 0.25 in. screens for sifting through the deposits, were typical of the archaeology of the day. Instead of contributing to the cultural history of the islands, the looted fishhooks went to private collections. Fishhooks from these private collections, stripped of the contextual information that might make them useful for the intellectual project started in the 1950s, are sometimes advertised for sale at online stores, where they are an ever-present reminder of an incompletely realized research opportunity.

Craft Production: Independent or Attached Specialists?

Burgeoning interests in socio-political development among Americanist archaeologists since the 1970s instigated a search for evidence of craft specialization, and archaeologists in Hawaiʻi followed suit by investigating stone adze technology and production in the archipelago (e.g., Cleghorn 1986; Lass 1994; McCoy 1990). Archaeologists in Hawaiʻi, like their colleagues in other world regions, assume that craft specialization is a correlate of early complex societies, and one that is accessible in the archaeological record (e.g., Costin 1991; Drennan and Peterson 2012:78; Lass 1998).

The large-scale production of stone adzes at the Mauna Kea Adze Quarry, near the highest summit of Hawaiʻi Island (Figure 5.7), is frequently interpreted as evidence of craft specialization (e.g., Cleghorn 1986; Kirch 1985; Mills et al. 2008; Williams 1989). With more than 265 workshops, 1,566

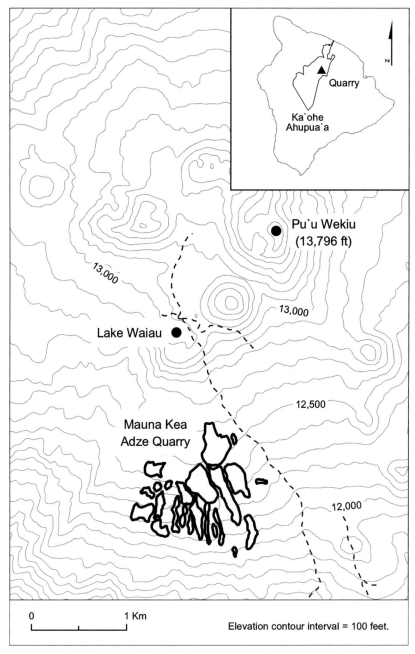

Figure 5.7: Mauna Kea adze quarry showing concentrated
deposits of adze-working debris.

chipping loci, 200 enclosures, 50 rockshelters, 45 shrines, and several petro-glyph panels over an area exceeding 12 km^2 (McCoy 1990:92–96; McCoy et al. 2009:446), this quarry was clearly a nexus of non-agricultural economic practice that was potentially orchestrated by a centralized and stratified system of leadership.

Archaeologist Paul Cleghorn (1982, 1986) conducted an innovative study of stone adze technology, production skill, and labor organization at Mauna Kea; his study entailed analyses of quarry debitage and experimental replication of adze reduction. In so doing, Cleghorn concludes that labor parties for adze production worked in teams of two individuals. Moreover, "expert craftsmen" practiced their craft in areas where high quality quarry material was abundant, whereas "novices or apprentices" worked with less valuable quarry material, to conserve the high quality material (McCoy 1999).

Although the intensity of stone adze production waned during the first century of contact (Bayman 2003), ethnohistoric observations corroborate the hypothesis of specialized production before contact. Statements by native Hawaiian historians, such as Malo (1951:51) who noted that "ax-makers were a greatly esteemed class," and Kamakau (1976:122) who acknowledged "the expert stoneworkers," imply that they were indeed craft specialists. The precise nature and consequences of such specialization has been an object of intensive archaeological study. Standardization in the style and metric morphology of Mauna Kea adzes signals highly specialized production to some scholars (e.g., Cleghorn 1986; Williams 1989), but not others (e.g., Lass 1994; McCoy 1990). Due to the logistical challenges of adze production in an inhospitable high-altitude setting (almost 4,267 m) like Mauna Kea, an elite-sponsored infrastructure was necessary (McCoy 1990) to sustain its system of "attached specialists" (Brumfiel and Earle 1987).

More recently, the emphasis on large-scale production at Mauna Kea has been balanced by the documentation of smaller quarries across the Hawaiian archipelago (e.g., Bayman and Moniz-Nakamura 2001; Kahn et al. 2009; Lass 1994; Mintmier 2007; Weisler 1990). Twelve quarry sites have been documented and geochemically characterized in the Hawaiian archipelago (Sinton and Sinoto 1997) and the number of known quarries, particularly smaller ones, is increasing as the pace of fieldwork has intensified (Figure 5.8).

Artisans at smaller quarries produced a wider range of tools for local consumers who resided within the same traditional territory (*ahupua'a*) (Leach 1993). Unlike adze-makers at Mauna Kea, artisans at smaller locales could be

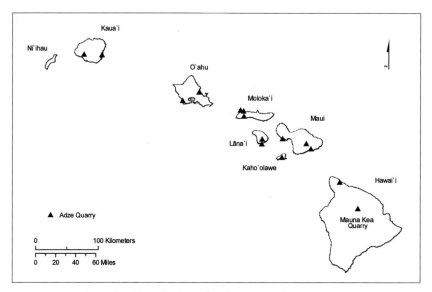

Figure 5.8: Distribution of major adze rock quarry sites.

characterized as "independent specialists" (Brumfiel and Earle 1987) who worked beyond the watchful gaze of Hawaiian chiefs or their administrative retinue (Bayman and Moniz-Nakamura 2001). Adzes at such locales were possibly made for expedient use as Hawaiians foraged the forested uplands for wood and plant fiber resources. However, at least some of the smaller quarries and adze production sites were possibly still linked with elites, albeit less directly.

For example, Hawaiians at a small adze production site at Pōhakuloa, on the upland saddle of Hawai'i Island (but below Mauna Kea), focused on a variety of activities, including abrader manufacturing and woodworking, as well as bird catching and bird cooking (Bayman and Moniz-Nakamura 2001:249). Hawaiian chiefs consumed juvenile birds, primarily petrels, and received feathers as tribute from commoners, and so the artisans at this locale may have been chiefly retainers, although ethnohistoric accounts are equivocal on this issue (Lass 1998:20). In either case, there was a god of "bird catchers ... and those who did feather-work" (Malo 1951:82).

Compositional Perspectives on Adze Circulation

Anthropologists and archaeologists once regularly invoked ethnohistoric accounts to argue that resources and goods circulated through centralized

78

systems of chiefly redistribution (Earle 1977; Sahlins 1972). Competing models of Hawaiian stone adze circulation, which may or may not include exchange, have been evaluated using technological analyses and a variety of artifact characterization techniques including petrography (Cleghorn et al. 1985; Lass 1994), destructive wave-length-dispersive X-ray fluorescence (WDXRF) analysis (e.g., Sinton and Sinoto 1997; Weisler 1990, 1998b), and non-destructive energy-dispersive X-ray fluorescence (EDXRF) analysis (e.g., Kahn et al. 2009; Lundblad et al. 2008; Mills et al. 2008, 2010; Kirch et al. 2012). Recent archaeological studies of the compositional characteristics of stone adzes confirm that their production was sometimes, but not always, centralized (e.g., Kahn et al. 2009), even in instances of highly specialized production.

For example, archaeologist Barbara Lass's (1998:25) technological study of 135 stone adzes from dated archaeological sites on Hawai'i Island detected uniformity in adze shape that was seemingly confounded by her petrographic analysis. Moreover, her technological study indicated that standardization did not increase over time, as earlier scholars once believed (e.g., nil Emory 1968:162–164; Kirch 1985:184–185). Instead, Lass (1998:25) argues that apparent "standardization" most likely reflects functional imperatives, such as specific hafting techniques, or cultural or stylistic norms that are not related to craft specialization (such as a controlled industry). This finding is echoed by her petrographic analysis of stone adzes from Hawai'i Island: they were made at a number of quarries besides Mauna Kea and they circulated widely, thus indicating (to her) a lack of centralized control by chiefly elites or craft specialists.

Lass's findings have since been complemented by other studies of Hawaiian stone adze production that confirm the use of local material in some instances (e.g., Bayman and Moniz-Nakamura 2001; Kahn et al. 2009; Weisler 2011). Conversely, a recent analysis on Maui confirms that basalt artifacts of fine-grained material that originated on O'ahu, Moloka'i, Lāna'i, and Hawai'i islands was most commonly deposited in elite residential features and in temple contexts (Kirch et al. 2012). This pattern is taken as support of a hypothesis of elite control of a "wealth economy" that included the circulation of high-quality, non-local stone before European contact. The circulation of lithic raw materials within and among islands has also been documented through geochemical studies of basalt on Kaua'i and Hawai'i Island (e.g., Mills et al. 2002; Mills et al. 2010). The circulation of such materials before and after contact was likely facilitated by the construction of paved trails that traversed historically documented *ahupua'a* territories (Mills 2002b).

In any event, archaeological evidence for both intra- and inter-island circulation of lithic material and/or finished adzes within the Hawaiian archipelago has been detected by geochemical studies. Moreover, geochemical evidence for the "export" of a Hawaiian adze to the Tuamotu Islands—approximately 2,500 km away—has been reported (Collerson and Weisler 2007), albeit from an undated context. This evidence for long-distance movement of stone adzes potentially complements oral traditions of round-trip voyages between Hawai'i and ancestral islands to the south at a time dated genealogically to the fourteenth century (Fornander 1996; Stokes 1933).

Of course, basalt was used to manufacture other artifacts that were used and circulated in precontact Hawai'i, including stone bowls (Lebo and Johnson 2007) and food processors, such as *poi* pounders (McElroy 2004). Compositional studies of such artifacts are still in their infancy, but they will eventually broaden understanding of the use and circulation of lithic resources across the archipelago. Production and use of stone bowls made with local basalt on the islands of Nihoa and Hā'ena (Necker) were indicated by a study using XRF and ICP-MS (Lebo and Johnson 2007). Of course, mechanisms behind the production and use of ritual objects like stone bowls were likely different than those that governed the use and circulation of stone adzes—especially those adzes that were used for mundane activities.

Featherwork Technology and Economy

The stunningly elaborate featherwork of traditional Hawaiian culture is one of its most celebrated hallmarks. Because Hawaiian featherwork was directly witnessed and documented by native Hawaiian writers and others during the post-contact period—and it is rarely preserved in archaeological contexts—scholarly treatment of its production and use is largely synchronic. The long-term development of this craft is therefore poorly understood, and yet it was an exceedingly important dimension of Hawaiian political economy in the post-contact period. Still, Kaeppler's (1985) study of featherwork indicates that it became increasingly uniform as Western influence became more pronounced.

Feather items were crafted with thousands of red, yellow, and black feathers that were acquired from various native birds (i.e., forest songbirds or honeycreepers). The color red was associated with gods throughout Polynesia; over time, however, a scarcity of red feathers was mitigated through their replacement with yellow feathers. Sumptuary restrictions governed access to Hawaiian featherwork, which consisted of elite garments and regalia such as cloaks, capes, helmets, standards (*kāhili*), necklaces (*lei*), and god images. Chiefs, kings, and other Hawaiian royalty enjoyed exclusive rights to feather objects which they accumulated through tribute and taxation of commoners during the *makahiki* season (Malo 1951:77).

Bird catching for the extraction of feathers was a male activity and it was conducted with the religious sanction of a specific god. The gender of those who practiced various kinds of featherwork is unclear; some sources reference the role of males (Kamakau 1976:123), whereas others highlight the involvement of women (Brigham 1899:26; Freycinet et al. 1978; see Linnekin 1988; see Lass 1994). Some accounts imply that featherwork was undertaken by Hawaiian elites (Byron 1826:9); if so, then perhaps feather workers were "embedded specialists" (Ames 1995) like ancient Maya elites who produced certain crafts to establish and maintain their political power (Inomata 2001). Alternatively, it is equally plausible that featherwork was undertaken by chiefly retainers who were commissioned as "attached specialists" (Lass 1994:21).

Although direct archaeological evidence of featherwork is lacking, detailed studies of museum collections of feather objects that were used in the eighteenth and nineteenth centuries (Buck 1957; Rose et al. 1993) underscore the astonishing investment of labor that their construction entailed. In one instance, a *kāhili* standard is estimated to have required as many as 11,360 feathers, from as many as 1,900 birds (Rose et al. 1993:300, Table 7). Even more remarkable, a magnificent yellow and red cloak that was worn by King Kamehahemeha I, in the early contact period, could have required as many 450,000 feathers that were secured from up to 80,000 rare birds (Buck 1957:231; Kirch 2010a).

Indirect and arguable archaeological and paleontological evidence of the deleterious consequences of bird catching for featherwork lies in the extinction of certain species of Hawaiian avifauna. Although bird catching possibly contributed to a decline in certain species, habitat disturbance from agricultural production and the effects of introduced predators, such as the Polynesian rat, probably played a more decisive role (Rose et al. 1993:299–301).

Conclusions

Questions surrounding the nature of craft production in pre-European Hawai'i remain unresolved. Although archaeological evidence of intensified stone adze production at Mauna Kea, the largest quarry in the Pacific region, is frequently invoked to support models of attached specialization in which the adze makers worked solely in the service of elites, it is quite plausible that it was practiced also by independent specialists in the service of both commoners and elites. The fact that the quarry lies within a single historically documented land division confounds arguments that it was controlled by an island-wide hierarchy of chiefly or kingly elites. In either case, recent studies of lithic raw material such as basalt and volcanic glass confirm that Hawaiian *ahupua'a* were not autonomous economic units. Instead, lithic raw materials, and perhaps other materials, circulated within and among different *ahupua'a* territories in pre-European Hawai'i (Kirch et al. 2012; M. McCoy 2011; Mills et al. 2011). Future research is necessary to determine whether the circulation of such resources was undertaken through direct procurement, down-the-line exchange, or other means of distribution (Renfrew 1977).

Moreover, the Hawaiian archaeological record rarely yields direct evidence of craft goods that were particularly vital to the political economy of the contact period, such as featherwork and barkcloth. Finely crafted featherwork and barkcloth materialized the political economy of class stratification in contact-period Hawai'i, and yet such goods are largely absent in the archaeological record of the precontact period.

In summary, archaeological and ethnohistorical research on Hawaiian craft economies during the past few decades has revealed the following findings: (i) the circulation of crafted goods and raw materials confirms that traditional Hawaiian territories were not economically autonomous; and (ii) crafted goods that visibly materialized class stratification in contact-period Hawai'i are rarely preserved in the archaeological record. In the next chapter we consider the broader implications of these findings for archaeological studies that purport to detect the presence of "primary states" in ancient Hawai'i.

6

Ideology and Political Economy

M ost archaeologists in the Hawaiian Islands are trained in the Americanist tradition of anthropological archaeology. Since the late 1960s much of their attention has focused on the development and operation of chiefdoms and early states, so-called "primitive" or "archaic" states. Unlike many of their colleagues in the Americas, however, Hawaii's archaeologists generally shunned the heated debates that stemmed from competing interpretations of sociopolitical development (i.e., "is it a complex chiefdom or an early state?"). This was partially due to their use of comparative Polynesian ethnology, which indicated to Hawaii's archaeologists that a high degree of class stratification developed in the islands from a founding population with a more egalitarian social structure. They followed their American colleagues, however, when they attempted to explain the rise of social stratification by the operation of "prime movers" such as population growth, social circumscription, warfare, or some combination of these.

Because Hawaii's archaeologists knew from comparative ethnology that the islands witnessed the development of highly stratified, complex societies, they charged themselves with the mission of documenting the expected archaeological correlates of this cultural phenomenon. Like their colleagues in the Americas (e.g., Flannery 1998), their research has typically focused on multi-scalar analyses of the archaeological correlates that index the sociopolitical control of labor with respect to (i) settlement patterns; (ii) subsistence intensification; (iii) craft specialization; (iv) monumentality; and (v) mortuary practices. Our discussion below outlines key dimensions of these topics as they relate to archaeological interpretations of traditional political economy in Hawai'i.

Settlement Patterns

As we noted in Chapter 4, Hawaii's earliest populations were concentrated around salubrious core areas which were favorable for shallow water inshore shellfishing and fishing and irrigation farming. These locales offered other vital resources including seaweed, wood, plant fiber, and birds. By the sixteenth century, most environments of the islands—both windward and leeward, and coastal and inland—were occupied and the territorial arrangement of Hawaii's contact-period populations was arguably established.

Contact-period residential settlements typically comprised one or more households; these households sometimes included multiple buildings and other features, such as earth ovens and canoe sheds. Although contact-period accounts reveal that gender was by then a fundamental organizing principle in traditional Hawaiian society—and that certain activities, such as eating, were gendered and spatially segregated—the development of this imperative is an under-studied topic of archaeology (but see Van Gilder 2001).

According to traditional accounts from the sixteenth century, Hawaii's islands were also divided into narrow territorial units called *ahupua'a* that typically crosscut ecological zones ranging from the coasts to the interior uplands. Other nested territorial divisions, both larger and smaller than *ahupua'a*, such as *moku* and *'ili*, are recalled in Hawaiian traditions. Archaeological correlates of some, but not all, territorial divisions have been proposed by archaeologists. Archaeological evidence of walls and trails, for example, seemingly mirror certain historically documented *ahupua'a*.

Subsistence Intensification

Our discussion in Chapter 4 of Hawaiian subsistence economies underscores the varied constraints and opportunities for the intensification of food production and resource extraction. Perhaps not surprisingly, agricultural intensification has received the most attention from Hawaii's archaeologists since its evidence is especially abundant on the islands' landscapes. Moreover, Hawaii's archaeologists share the long-standing conviction of scholars elsewhere in the world that agricultural intensification paralleled, if not caused, the emergence and proliferation of complex societies, since it, among other things, sustained the production of surplus food that was used by elites to finance the political economy through systems of tribute and feasting.

Accordingly, Hawaii's archaeologists take note of evidence that agricultural production expanded until ca. A.D. 1600, when all but the most marginal locales were under cultivation. From that point forward, a relentless trajectory of intensification ensued until a few decades after European contact, but before Hawaiian populations plummeted from disease epidemics.

Hawaii's subsistence and political economies were strengthened with aquaculture, wherein fish like mullet were husbanded in large, labor-intensive artificial ponds that were constructed on coastal reefs. Oral traditions and limited chronometric dating of fishponds imply that they were mostly constructed after the fourteenth century. By European contact, such facilities operated under the purview of chiefly oversight.

The hypothesis that bird-nesting habitat was enhanced through anthropogenic alteration of the Hawaiian landscape, through the excavation of shallow pits, remains to be well substantiated. Unlike the honeycreeper birds that were exploited for their colorful feathers, petrels were foraged for their fat and protein. Nonetheless, ethnohistoric accounts reveal that both kinds of birds were a prerogative of high-ranking elites. The substantiation of the bird husbandry hypothesis—and confirmation that it was contemporaneous with the emergence of class stratification—would greatly enrich archaeological models of Hawaiian political economy.

Craft Specialization

Traditional Hawaiian craft specialization was unrivaled in comparison with other Polynesian societies, and it is well documented in ethnohistoric sources and, to a far lesser extent, archaeology. As we noted in Chapter 5, some of the most elaborate expressions of craft specialization during the post-contact period were focused on perishable media such as feathers and wood. The extraordinary role of feather regalia, such as cloaks, helmets, and standards, in materializing elite identity and power during the contact period has long captured the public imagination, and yet, such perishable items are beyond the purview of scholars who focus on materials preserved in the archaeological record.

Instead, because stone adzes are so well preserved in the archaeological record, and they were so vital in Hawaiian society, they have received the lion's share of attention by pre-historians. Since stone adzes were used for elite-sponsored activities, such as the clearance of forests for agriculture, the construction of war canoes, and the erection of religious temples, they linked the subsistence economy and the political economy (Lass 1994). Although scholars agree that stone adzes were fundamental in precontact Hawai'i, interpreting the organization of their production and circulation is a nexus of ongoing debate. Put simply, the question of whether the production and circulation of adzes at the largest quarries, such as Mauna Kea, were undertaken by either attached or independent specialists has not been answered satisfactorily. Moreover, the question of whether adzes from the relatively small-scale quarries were mostly used locally within a single *ahupua'a* territory, or widely circulated beyond an *ahupua'a* territory, is also a topic of ongoing investigation.

Still, because intensification of stone adze production coincided with the expansion of agriculture and temple construction across the archipelago, stone adzes are often invoked in archaeological models of Hawaiian political economy.

Monumentality

Traditional Hawaiian religious temples are today visible in the archaeological record of their stone foundations and walls, and their associated offerings of coral and/or remains of pig and/or human bone (Figure 6.1). Detailed studies of ethnohistoric accounts of Hawaiian temples and their archaeological manifestations confirm great variability in both their ritual functions and their material morphology. Temples in traditional Hawaiian society ranged from solitary upright stones to large complexes of perishable pole-and-thatch buildings and other features, such as wooden towers and platforms for sacrificial offerings. Despite the variability in their precise functions, morphology, and size, all Hawaiian temples were locales for the delivery of offerings and sacrifices to the god(s).

Although it has proven profoundly challenging to classify Hawaiian temples (Valeri 1985a), the operating assumption among archaeologists is that one class of temples was dedicated to gods of fertility and production, such as Lono, whereas another class of temples was focused on honoring Kū, the god of war. Moreover, researchers distinguish between modest temples that were used for worship by relatively small groups of individuals, such as the shrines for fishermen typically found near the shore or the shrine used by males in a household, and the larger war temples that figured in polity-wide

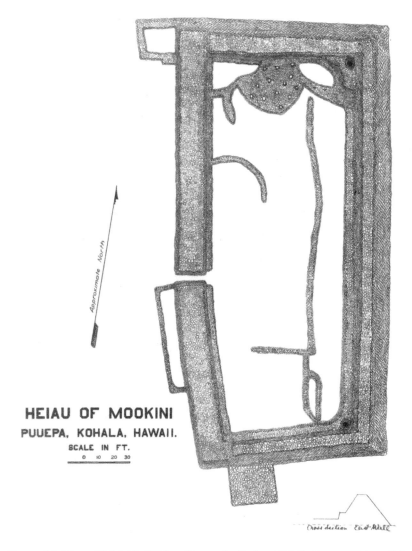

Figure 6.1: Map of Moʻokini Heiau. Drawn by Stokes (1991). Source: Heiau of the Island of Hawaiʻi, Bishop Museum Press, 1991. Reprinted with permission.

rituals that might include human sacrifice among other offerings (Figure 6.2). In the early contact period, before the traditional Hawaiian religion was terminated in 1819, rituals at war temples sanctioned conquest warfare and commemorated chiefly succession.

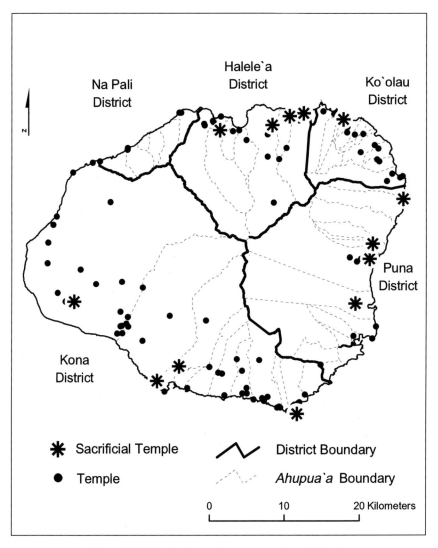

Figure 6.2: Distribution of temples on Kaua'i Island.

Archaeological excavation of Hawaiian temples, especially the larger *luakini*, has been relatively limited (e.g., Kolb 1994; Ladd 1973, 1985). Nonetheless, studies confirm that some Hawaiian temples were constructed, redesigned, and elaborated over many generations, and that their functions varied across time. Some temples, for example, were originally constructed to worship Lono, presumably to enhance fertility and production, and then later reconfigured to worship the war god, Kū. Archaeological signatures of the dynamic use of Hawaiian religious temples, in tandem with traditional accounts, offer tantalizing insights on the political machinations that prevailed in traditional society. Such perspectives inform the alternative models of Hawaiian political economy that we consider below.

Mortuary Practices

Archaeologists who work in Hawai'i have not detected conventional mortuary evidence for social inequality and hierarchical political organization that typically characterizes early complex societies (nil Flannery 1998:46–57): rich grave good assemblages and great investments of labor in the construction of tombs or other mortuary facilities are generally absent in the Hawaiian archaeological record. Yet, ironically, this pattern, in tandem with ethnohistoric records, offers negative evidence of social inequality. Ethnohistoric accounts by native Hawaiians in the early post-contact period reveal that the remains of high-ranking individuals were often hidden to protect their spiritual power from desecration by their enemies. Indeed, the most powerful ruler in Hawaiian history, Kamehameha I, who conquered the archipelago seventeen years after European contact, remains buried in secrecy to this day. Consequently, the uppermost socio-political stratum in traditional Hawaiian society is archaeologically "invisible" for most of the chronological sequence in the archipelago. In contrast, Hawaiian commoners may be overrepresented in the archaeological record, giving the false impression that elites were exceedingly few in number and that traditional society was extraordinarily stratified.

Hawaiian mortuary treatment was quite varied and included interment in sand dunes or in sediments found inside caves, below domestic houses, below stone mounds, platforms, or other monuments, and inside religious temples, in addition to cremation. Human remains were occasionally curated in woven anthropomorphic caskets (Buck 1957:575), and some writers assert that there were two royal mausoleums on Hawai'i Island. According to an ethnohistoric account recorded in 1825 (Bloxam 1925), multiple kings and chiefs were interred in a temple called Hale-o-Keawe. Notably, this royal mausoleum (Buck 1957) comprised a thatched hut atop a stone pavement (Bloxam 1925). Among the bones were a variety of perishable Hawaiian materials, including carved wooden idols, barkcloth, calabashes containing shells and fishhooks, a small model of a canoe, two native drums, an English drum, and a Chinese mask (Bloxam 1925:74–76). Pieces of flax sailcloth of probable European origin, along with pieces of metal, were found in an extraordinary anthropomorphic basketry casket (Rose 1992:41ff.). The inclusion of European and Chinese goods with the bones is curious and hints that at least some, if not all, of the human interments and their associated offerings in the tomb postdate the inception of Hawaiian trade with Canton, China, in the early 1790s.

An early attempt to document class stratification by comparing energetic investments among burials in platforms, caves, and crevices in North Kona, Hawai'i Island (Tainter 1973, 1991; Tainter and Cordy 1977) was unfortunately limited by a lack of temporal control. Although grave goods are not commonly encountered in Hawaiian archaeology, documented materials include wood canoe hulls, bowls, and god images; barkcloth; *Pandanus* mats; fishing gear; chipped stone; faunal remains; and the unique insignia of high rank, the whale tooth pendant, which was made from clam shell and a variety of other materials in addition to whale teeth. Most notably, the discovery of insignia with both children and adults offers tantalizing evidence of ascribed status.

However, a detailed analysis (Donham 2000:8.18–8.19) of mortuary materials at Honokahua, Maui, revealed three key findings: (i) the graves of most elite individuals did not exhibit high degrees of energy expenditure; (ii) the burials of most elites did not have rich grave good assemblages; and (iii) the graves of elite individuals were not spatially segregated from non-elite commoners. The implications of these findings include the following: (i) the archaeological correlates of class stratification that scholars expect to find in complex societies are lacking in Hawaii's mortuary record; and (ii) the Hawaiian mortuary record does not support the assertion of many scholars that kinship ties between elites and commoners were irrevocably severed in the seventeenth century.

If stratification did indeed develop before contact, it is not evidenced in the Hawaiian archaeological record of mortuary behavior. This pattern distinguishes the Hawaiian case study from other early complex societies and archaic states that scholars have documented elsewhere in the world (e.g., Flannery 1998:46–57).

Conflict and Warfare

Conflict and warfare are commonly featured in discussions of ancient Hawaiian political economy (e.g., Kirch 2010a; Kolb and Dixon 2002; Wolforth 2005). These models stem from analyses of oral traditions (e.g., Fornander 1996) and post-contact-period accounts (Kamakau 1964; Malo 1951) of pervasive conflict and warfare in Hawaiian society. Such models seemingly adopt—a priori—the tantalizing assumption that oral traditions recall specific historical people and events. These narratives of conquest warfare in the two centuries prior to Cook's arrival in A.D. 1778 are invoked as supporting evidence for the emergence of secular kings who ruled as many as three different states in the Hawaiian archipelago (e.g., Kirch 2010a). Arguments for conquest warfare in ancient Hawai'i appear to be confounded by ethnohistoric reports of places of refuge, where endangered warriors and non-combatants could secure sacred protection from physical attack. The documentation of no less than 49 such facilities on Hawai'i Island (Kolb and Dixon 2002:523) implies that warfare in the islands was a ritual activity, unlike the more secular conquest warfare that was practiced in some early state societies.

Archaeological manifestations of warfare in Hawai'i and elsewhere potentially include fortifications and buffer zones, weapons, skeletal trauma, burned settlements, and/or militaristic iconography (e.g., Keeley 1996; LeBlanc 1999; Webster 1998:315). The archaeological correlates of warfare in Hawaiian oral traditions and contact-period accounts are disappointingly scarce, however, in comparison to the archaeological records of other societies in Oceania, such as New Zealand, and the Americas, such as the Mississippian and Southwestern cultures in the United States (Kolb and Dixon 2002:528–530).

In contact-period Hawai'i, weapons such as spears, clubs, and strangling cords were often fabricated with wood and cordage, which are perishable and rarely recovered in the archaeological record (Buck 1957), although stone clubs and slingstones are occasionally reported. Moreover, strong evidence of fortifications in Hawai'i is lacking and documented examples of skeletal trauma are exceedingly rare. Fortifications are the costliest and largest features of pre-industrial military technology, and only a few states in the world lacked them (Keeley 1996:55). The dearth of material correlates of Hawaiian warfare (Kirch 1990:339) stands in stark contrast with the archaeological record of violence and warfare in ancient Mississippian (e.g., Dye 2006) and Southwestern societies (e.g., LeBlanc 1999) in the continental United States, and many other world regions.

By way of comparison, excavations at the Crow Creek site in South Dakota, near the Missouri River, revealed the remains of 486 bodies in an incomplete palisade-and-ditch fortification, as well as other bodies in nearby burned lodges (Pauketat 2005). Victims of the attack included men, women, and children who had been dispatched with arrows and clubs and then burned. Mutilation of many bodies was typical and included, but was not limited to, decapitation and dismemberment. Other variants of violence—including cannibalism—are well documented in the American Southwest (e.g. Turner and Turner 1999; White 1992).

Thus, although conflict and warfare were possibly a fundamental feature of Hawaiian political economy and the rise of archaic or primary states before European contact, it has not yet been substantiated in the archaeological record, despite more than a century of detailed fieldwork in the archipelago. Some writers (e.g., Hommon 2010:24–27; Kirch 2010a:69–74, 210–217) have argued that increasing population density in Hawai'i in late prehistory, in the face of limited land and a ceiling on agricultural production intensification, instigated conquest warfare on its crowded islands. Population pressure potentially encouraged competition and conflict in Hawai'i in precontact times, but such a pattern is at odds with the findings of cross-cultural analyses that indicate that there is no correlation between the frequency of warfare and the density of human population (Keeley 1996:118). Ironically, abundant ethnohistoric accounts of Hawaiian warfare echo a worldwide, historical trend, wherein the incidence and ferocity of lethal combat immediately escalated with the onset of Western contact and expansion (see Ferguson 2006) and the adoption of European armament.

The Dominant Archaeological Narrative

The rich legacy of anthropological scholarship on sociopolitical developments in Polynesia and the Hawaiian Islands is widely acknowledged by archaeologists in the Americas. Some of the seminal anthropological models (e.g., Sahlins 1972; Service 1962) of political economy that were formulated in Oceania many decades ago—such as chieftainship and redistribution—have been adopted by archaeologists throughout the world. The integration of archaeology, ethnography, ethnohistory, and oral traditions is another hallmark of conventional research in the Hawaiian archipelago.

In our discussion below, we sketch the broad outlines of the narrative that has dominated interpretations of Hawaii's ancient political economy. As we noted earlier, archaeologists have constructed the conventional narrative through the selective calibration of archaeological correlates of political economy, such as craft specialization and monumentality, with the particulars of ethnography and traditional knowledge.

Early Chiefdoms

Following conventional Oceanic archaeology, the first Polynesians to settle Hawai'i brought a pre-existing cultural system for organizing their ideology and political economy. This system is known to Oceanic specialists as "Ancestral Polynesian Society" (APS). The scholarly construction of APS over a period of several decades (Kirch and Green 2001) focused on using archaeology, ethnography, and linguistics to infer the material and intangible characteristics of a seminal "Polynesian" culture. Polynesian culture seemingly crystallized around 500 B.C. in the islands of the Western Polynesian archipelagos known today as Tonga and Samoa after they were initially settled by earlier populations of the archaeologically defined Lapita culture, known for its dentate-stamped ceramics, which are widespread in the Western Pacific.

Material correlates of APS, documented through excavations at dozens of archaeological sites, include plain-ware ceramics, distinctive fishhooks, and other artifacts. Kirch and Green (2001) have inferred less tangible dimensions of APS, including ideology and political economy, through semantic analyses of Polynesian vocabulary and their arguably successful calibration with the archaeological record and ethnographic texts. The highly detailed picture of early Polynesian culture produced by this procedure is beyond the scope of this review.

Key elements of the Kirch and Green (2001) model are, however, relevant to the interpretation of early Hawaiian ideology and political economy: (i) exogamous landholding groups traced their genealogical descent (or ascent) from founding ancestor(s); (ii) such groups were administered by senior males who inherited their positions within the highest ranking lineages; (iii) these hereditary rulers served as both secular and ritual leaders;

(iv) leaders legitimated through their rule by ritually mediating the transmission of supernatural power from founding ancestors to living communities; and (v) such rites were anchored to an annual lunar calendar and undertaken at religious temples.

Direct archaeological evidence of this linguistic construction of APS is generally absent in the Hawaiian Islands; ceramics, for example, were not made or used in this part of Oceania. Nonetheless, archaeologists in Hawai'i typically assume, or imply, that early settlers in the archipelago organized themselves as corporate kin groups that held community lands in partnership with their ruling chiefs (Cordy 2004:2; Hommon 1986). Because such groups comprised kin, power was not highly concentrated within polities and endogamous class stratification was absent.

Material correlates of this political economy are essentially negative: the archaeological record of this early period prior to ca. A.D. 1400 offers limited evidence of agricultural intensification, craft specialization, large-scale monumentality, and/or elaborate mortuary practices. Indeed, as discussed in Chapter 3, well-dated archaeological evidence for this early period is extremely slight. Moreover, human populations were relatively small during the earlier part of this period (Dye and Komori 1992) and settlements were concentrated in the most favorable economic environments of the islands: areas along the coasts that were productive for farming and fishing (Hommon 1986).

Emergence of States

Scholarly interpretations of early states in the Hawaiian archipelago have long emphasized the integration of archaeological information with ethnohistoric accounts and oral traditions compiled during the late eighteenth and early nineteenth centuries (e.g., Hommon 1986; Kirch 2010a). Such accounts have provided prehistorians independent sources of information to infer the past, and enliven and humanize their interpretations of a silent archaeological record.

Eyewitness accounts in the first decades following contact describe the daily lives and political machinations of elites and, to a lesser extent, commoners in no fewer than four multi-island polities. The configuration of the polities was dynamic, and their control changed hands frequently and rapidly in the face of endemic warfare. Hawaiian sociopolitical structure reached an apex of transformation when Kamehameha united the islands of the archipelago into a single kingdom in 1810.

Written accounts between contact in 1778 and inter-island unification in 1810 describe a highly stratified society. Hawaiian polities were centralized, hierarchical, and sharply divided into endogamous social classes. Hawaiian polities were administered through a series of nested territorial units, subsistence emphasized the production of a surplus, craft economies were deployed to materialize elite status, and rituals at temples were exercised to legitimate divine kings. Within the annual cycle, religious rites rotated between temples dedicated to one of two of the four major deities of the Hawaiian pantheon: Lono, the god of dryland agriculture; and Kū, the god of war.

Most notably, rulers in contact-period Hawaiian society were divine kings. Kings traced long and venerable genealogies, whereas commoners were expressly prohibited from tracking their genealogies back in deep time. Commoners no longer enjoyed inherent rights to particular plots of land as members of lineages; they worked it at the pleasure of kings to whom they paid tribute.

To some archaeologists, eyewitness accounts of Hawaiian polities in the contact period confirm the presence of "primary" or "pristine" state societies. The central question that remains, therefore, is the following: why and when did states emerge in the Hawaiian Islands? Successfully answering this question requires anthropological archaeology.

Archaeological models of the emergence of early states in Hawai'i have emphasized the expansion and intensification of agricultural production in the wake of growing populations and demographic pressure (e.g., Allen 1991; Cordy 1981; Hommon 1986). Expansion of agricultural production to less favorable inland areas on the leeward sides of the islands generally focused on crops such as sweet potato and yams that required less water than the preferred staple, taro. Once the most arable areas of the islands were under cultivation, the territorial communities known as *ahupua'a* presumably crystallized (Hommon 1986).

Although direct archaeological evidence of the consequence of *ahupua'a* communities is lacking, many scholars infer that they were fundamental administrative units of Hawaiian society, both before and after contact. The precise chronological timing of agricultural expansion and intensification is an unresolved—and profoundly important—question because of its implications for the rise of early states in Hawai'i.

Some scholars argue that population growth was paralleled by agricultural expansion and intensification that began early in the fifteenth century and reached its apex in the mid-seventeenth century (Kirch 2011:128, Table 4.1). Chronometric evidence suggests that investment in the construction of monumental temples—and the construction of palace-like residences—coincided with the trajectory of agricultural intensification and the rise of powerful kings who presided over emergent states (Kirch 2010a).

The chronometric analyses that sustain arguments for the emergence of early states in the mid-seventeenth century are, however, equivocal and fraught with uncertainty. A detailed reanalysis of chronometric dates from the Leeward Kohala field system, a large agricultural field system on Hawai'i Island, indicates that a significant fraction of intensification and, according to the model, early state formation, transpired during the first few decades of the nineteenth century (Dye 2011b). While this finding does not preclude the possibility that early states did indeed emerge in Hawai'i in the mid-seventeenth or even the eighteenth century, the precise timing of their rise remains to be confirmed by future research. Confirmation of the timing of agricultural intensification and early state emergence in the Hawaiian Islands is essential for determining whether they were examples of primary states that developed before contact with Europeans, or secondary states that arose after contact. Resolving this question is fundamental to understanding why early states emerged in the Hawaiian archipelago.

Implications of the Hawaiian Example

The development of ancient complex societies in the Hawaiian archipelago challenges anthropological archaeology with respect to two closely related issues: (i) the conceptualization of "states" per se; and (ii) the utility of the correlate method (Drennan and Peterson 2012:72–79) for their discovery and interpretation. Generations of scholars working throughout the world have problematized the conceptualization of ancient states and the characteristics that distinguish them from other complex non-state societies, such as chiefdoms (Yoffee 2005). Questions have also been raised about the correlate method. According to Norman Yoffee, when scholars have used the correlate method, the "'archaeological' procedure was to correlate one or more central features of a favorite ethnographic type with some excavated material, then extrapolate all the rest of the characteristics of the type and so bring the not-directly-observable dimensions of ancient society into view" (Yoffee 2005:23). Ironically, the Hawaiian example offers a particularly challenging conundrum because its early states were well documented by ethnohistory, and yet, the archaeological correlates that are often construed to typify such societies are generally absent or ambiguous in the Hawaiian Islands. For example, robust archaeological evidence of urbanism, long-distance trade, elaborate mortuary programs, and labor-intensive monumentality is generally absent, rare, or equivocal in Hawai'i.

In Chapter 5, for example, we noted that some Hawaiian craft objects— such as those made with feathers or wood—are not normally preserved in the archaeological record, and yet they materialized the Hawaiian political economy of class stratification. Moreover, it is apparent from both archaeology and ethnohistory that particular cultural imperatives precluded the development of highly elaborate, labor-intensive mortuary programs. Quite often, for example, the remains of elite males were hidden to prevent their desecration by those who might work them into fishhooks or other implements.

Finally, although some Hawaiian temples were sizable, some of the most important ones were relatively small in scale and labor investment (Hommon 2010). Indeed, high population levels in the late pre-contact period meant that ever smaller fractions of the total population were required to construct such temples. Hawaiian religious performances generated an archaeological record of temples that does not exceed or even match the scale of many early state and non-state temples that archaeologists have documented elsewhere in the world; in short, monumental architecture in Hawai'i is not so "monumental" (Table 6.1).

Thus, a fundamental finding of the Hawaiian example is that conventional use of the correlate method by anthropological archaeologists to discover and characterize the development of ancient states is inherently limited. Other ancient states in the world, including North America, have likely been overlooked because their archaeological records, like Hawaii's, do not manifest the material correlates that anthropological archaeologists typically expect to recover. In the exceptional case of Hawai'i, however, contact-period historical records counterbalance the limitations of a more conventional anthropological approach to the archaeology of complex societies. And yet, the early historical records often describe events and processes triggered by Hawaii's contact with Europeans and Americans that intensified class stratification and inequality (Kirch and Sahlins 1992:I 49ff., 82–83). These pressures were suf-

Table 6.1: Selected Archaeological Monuments in Hawaiʻi and North America.

Monument	Construction Time Span	Monument Type	Area (m²)	Selected sources
Hawaiian				
Piʻilanihale	A.D. 1400–1650	Temple, residence	12,126	Kolb (2012, 1994)
Loʻaloʻa	A.D. 1400–1650	Temple, residence	4,160	Kirch (2010a:158)
Moʻokini	A.D. 1400–1650	Temple	3,002	Cordy (2000:284) Kirch (2010a:170)
Hohokam				
Mesa Grande	A.D. 1200–1350	Temple, residence	14,045	Doelle et al. (1995:393)
Pueblo Grande	A.D. 1200–1350	Temple, residence	11,884	Doelle et al. (1995:393)
Las Colinas	A.D. 1200–1350	Temple, residence	12,956	Doelle et al. (1995:393)
Mississippian				
Moundville, Mound B	A.D. 1225–1300	Temple, residence	5,058	Pauketat (2007:118–123)
Etowah, Mound A	A.D. 1150–1375	Temple, residence	12,000	Pauketat (2007:115–117)
Monks Mound, Cahokia	A.D. 1050–1250	Temple, residence	64,750	Fowler (1975)

Note: Area statistics for Hawaiian and Hohokam monuments include their enclosing compounds.

ficiently intense that some scholars believe them responsible for creating features of the state that archaeologists seek in the traditional past (e.g., Andrade 2008:69; MacKenzie 1991; Osorio 2002:83).

Accordingly, anthropological archaeologists must refine and strengthen their use of the correlate method—and a "bottom-up" approach—so that an enlarged number of early states can be discovered and more fully characterized. The Hawaiian example offers the rare opportunity to independently examine the archaeological record from the perspective of historical records. The message is clear: not all states produced the conventional material correlates of urbanism, long-distance exchange, elaborate mortuary programs, and labor-intensive monumentality. Indeed, some states lacked these characteristics altogether.

7
Western Contact and Colonialism

Archaeological studies of contact and colonialism have emphasized the Americas (e.g., Deagan 1988; Spielmann et al. 2006), but other locales, such as Oceania, have experienced increasing attention (e.g., Chatan 2003; Fitzpatrick et al. 2006). Hawaii's contact with the West in the late eighteenth century was relatively late compared to the Americas, which first encountered Europeans in the late fifteenth century. This delay of almost three centuries enhances the study of contact between Hawai'i and the West; detailed documentary accounts, artistic illustrations, and photographic images of traditional lifeways and technologies were compiled within the first century.

Following British naval officer Captain James Cook's visit in A.D. 1778–1779, indigenous Hawaiians witnessed changes in their health, technologies, and society through the nineteenth century. The arrival of foreign disease pathogens, Western materials and technologies, and Christian ideologies altered traditional ways of life. Archaeological research offers insights on this historic transformation, but with a few notable exceptions (e.g., Carter 1990; Garland 1996; Kirch and Sahlins 1992; Mills 2002a; Six 2005; Sweeney 1992), research in Hawai'i has focused on the precontact period. This chapter considers the implications of archaeological and documentary evidence that traditional stone adze technology persisted long after European contact and the introduction of metal in A.D. 1778 (Bayman 2003). The ideological, political, and economic factors that underlay this dynamic process within a context of emergent colonialism are explored. To put this particular instance of technological change into a broader context, differential rates of adoption of Western clothing by indigenous Hawaiian women and changes in the design and construction of vernacular architecture are also acknowledged.

Social constructionist views of technological change are integrated with post-colonial concepts of *hybridity* in this chapter. Because social identities are materialized through technology, historical archaeology offers anthropology an opportunity to document economic and political dimensions of hybridity in colonial contexts (Lawrence and Shepherd 2006:71–75). Despite debate over Bhabha's particular conception of hybridity (Bhabha 1994; Friedman 1995:73, 80–85; Young Leslie and Addo 2007), it is a widely acknowledged consequence of colonial engagement.

In this chapter we consider three categories of material culture—stone adzes, women's clothing, and vernacular architecture—to highlight the various factors that underlie expressions of hybrid identity among post-contact Hawaiians. To situate this process in a broader context, we first provide a brief historical review of the archipelago in the eighteenth and nineteenth centuries.

Technological Change and Social Identity

As we noted in Chapter 6, Hawai'i had the most complex hierarchical organization and largest scale of economic production among traditional Polynesian societies at contact (Hommon 1986; Kirch 2000:300, 2010a). The eight major islands of the Hawaiian archipelago were divided into four polities at European contact; these polities have since been described as "complex chiefdoms" (e.g., Cordy 1981; Earle 1977) and "archaic" states (e.g., Hommon 1986:55; Kirch 2000:300, 2010a). Contact-period Hawaiian polities were highly stratified and pyramidal: they centered on high chiefs and administrators of local territorial communities, and included commoner subjects.

Throughout the late 1700s and early 1800s, the pace of technological change accelerated, beginning with Cook's supply of metal adzes. With the support of Western military technology and tactics, King Kamehameha I united the archipelago by 1810 (Kuykendall 1938:44–51). From that moment, a succession of indigenous kings and other elites and their commoner subjects were drawn into the rapidly expanding world system of economic interaction that included the export of sandalwood to China (Daws 2006:37).

In 1819, the dissolution of the traditional Hawaiian religion included the abolition of sumptuary restrictions that once prevented Hawaiian women from eating pork, certain varieties of bananas, and other foods (Kuykendall 1938:61). Shortly afterward, Christian missionaries from the

United States brought Western clothing styles while the island economy continued to change. After 1830, the sandalwood trade was replaced by an economy that centered on the production of provisions such as pork and yams for whalers who plied the waters of the Pacific between 1830 and 1860 (Daws 2006:119–120).

Although ruling Hawaiians initially benefited from this international economy, their power waned following the *Māhele* land reform of 1848–1850, which created a market for the sale of land (Kuykendall 1938:269–298). As an imbalance in international trade escalated and elite debts mounted, many Hawaiians lost their land and the effects of colonialism intensified. In 1893, Hawaii's reigning ruler, Queen Liliʻuokalani, and the constitutional monarchy of the Hawaiian Kingdom were overthrown by insurgents supported by US troops. Only a few years passed before the archipelago was annexed as a Territory of the United States in 1898. These historical events and their technological consequences are documented in the archaeological and documentary records of the post-contact period.

Stone adzes are an intriguing instance of technological persistence after contact with Europeans. Although some writers opine that stone adzes were less desirable than their metal counterparts (e.g., McCoy 1990:92–93; Oliver 2002), archaeological research indicates that this view might oversimplify a complex and gradual process (Cobb 2003:12). What was the impact of European metal on the traditional stone adze economy in the Hawaiian islands?

Stone Adzes

Stone adzes were used in Hawaiʻi for felling trees, building canoes and houses, carving religious idols (Kamakau 1976), tilling agricultural fields (Dockall 2000), and perhaps to display *mana* or rank, as they were in other areas of Polynesia (Leach 1993:39).

Archaeologists have long recognized the value of stone adzes in precontact Polynesian societies (e.g., Buck et al. 1930; Cleghorn 1986; Duff 1959; Emory 1968), and yet they rarely study the use of stone tools in post-contact Hawaiʻi (but see Kirch and Sahlins 1992). This trend is a notable contrast with areas in the Pacific region, like New Guinea and Australia, where studies of the impact of European metal on indigenous stone tool use have revealed its rich cultural meaning (e.g., Salisbury 1962; Sharp 1952). The lack of attention to post-contact stone adze economies in the Hawaiian islands clearly contributes to the "rapid replacement" view of some archaeologists (e.g., McCoy 1990:92–93) and historians (e.g., Kuykendall 1938). This "rapid replacement" view reflects assumptions of economic efficiency. Indeed, the greater efficiency of metal tools for cutting trees and carving wood has been repeatedly documented (e.g., Mathieu and Meyer 1997; Townsend 1969).

Nineteen post-contact archaeological sites with stone adzes have been reported in the Hawaiian Islands (Bayman 2003:103–104). Of course, it is possible that some sites dated with chronometric techniques actually reflect precontact occupations. Still, the recovery of stone adzes from some sites that also have European artifacts indicates that certain facets of traditional Hawaiian technology persisted long after contact with Europeans and Americans. In fact, a couple of rural sites on the island of O'ahu yielded traditional stone adzes in occupations as recent as A.D. 1880. Other post-contact sites with stone adzes are probably present in isolated rural settings, but such occupations are difficult to date since they often lack historic-period artifacts.

Some ancient stone adzes may have been kept as heirlooms, or recycled for other purposes. However, documentary accounts attest to continued stone adze use among commoners until the mid-nineteenth century (Cheever 1851). For example, in the late nineteenth century William Brigham noted the following:

> In watching the shaping of a canoe I have seen the old canoe-maker use for the rough shaping and excavating an ordinary foreign steel adze, but for the finishing touches he dropped the foreign tool and returned to the adze of his ancestors, and the blunt looking stone cut off a delicate shaving from the very hard koa wood and never seemed to take too much as the foreign adze was apt to do. (Brigham 1902:409–410)

Brigham (1902:408, 415) added that while the production of stone adzes eventually terminated after the introduction of metal, their use continued at least as late as 1864. Brigham's statements also imply that certain "performance characteristics" (sensu Schiffer 2004) of stone adzes, such as their use for intricate carving, illustrate a concern with aesthetics by canoe artisans. In this respect, the decline of canoe-making aesthetics in the late nineteenth century was noted by John Cobb in 1900:

> the older ones [canoes] are very handsome in design and workmanship, the old-time native boat builders having been especially expert in their manufacture. The present generation has sadly deteriorated, however, and the canoes made now by natives rarely show very much skill in design and workmanship. (Holmes 1981:42)

Although the eventual adoption of metal adzes by virtually all Hawaiians contributed to a decline in the aesthetic quality of canoe artisanship, some islands, and certain areas of islands, acquired them more quickly than others. The observation that stone adzes were "becoming rare" in Honolulu by 1825 (Byron 1826:137) is not surprising because Honolulu was a major port. Rural districts remained isolated from the market economy until the middle of the nineteenth century (Linnekin 1990:173), about 25 years after stone adzes had almost disappeared in Honolulu. In the settlement of Waimea, located in the interior of the island of Hawai'i, stone adze use was witnessed as late as 1847 (Doyle 1953:145). Archaeological evidence demonstrates that stone adzes were still used in other remote districts and islands without major seaports, such as Moloka'i (McElroy 2007:113).

There are also indications that iron was differentially distributed between elites and commoners. Chiefs used their traditional prerogatives to control the use of foreign materials by commoners (Linnekin 1990:161). In the late 1700s, Nathaniel Portlock witnessed a chief demand bits of iron from a commoner who had acquired them from foreigners (Linnekin 1990:162; Portlock 1968 [1789]). Although by 1793 chiefs had "more iron than they knew what to do with" (Bell 1929), commoners still sought the material, especially nails and scissors. The eagerness of commoners to gain access to such materials in the late eighteenth century implies that iron was scarce for them because its distribution was controlled by elites. In short, economic and social factors contributed to the persistence of stone adze technology after contact with Europeans and Americans. Stone adzes were valued by canoe artisans who operated, in some cases, under the purview of elites. Even if stone adzes had not been valued by canoe artisans, commoners were often compelled to use them, especially in rural areas where metal adzes were difficult to acquire. In all cases, the persistence of stone adze technology was tied to a political economy that emphasized elite prestige and power. Whether or not elites controlled metal adzes consciously to link their identity with Europeans, their success in doing so underscores their power over commoner Hawaiians who also sought Western goods and materials. Unlike metal, access to Western clothing styles was quickly available to commoners who were encouraged to wear them by Christian missionaries in the early nineteenth century.

Barkcloth Garments

Throughout the world, clothing is used for asserting ethnicity, gender, class, and other dimensions of identity and social control (e.g., Arthur 1999; Barber 1994; Costin and Wright 1998; Murra 1962; Weiner and Schneider 1989; Wobst 1977). Materials for making clothing are often locally available, they are relatively light and easy to transport, and are amenable to stylistic elaboration. For these reasons, clothing can be an effective medium of nonverbal communication. Such visual means of communication were essential in colonial societies (Pels 1997:169); nineteenth-century Hawai'i was no exception.

Before the arrival of American Congregationalist missionaries in 1820, most Hawaiians wore barkcloth garments, except for Hawaiian elites who had acquired Western garments from Cook and others and Chinese silk as early as 1810. Elites also adorned themselves with bright colored feather clothing and paraphernalia including cloaks, helmets, and *kāhili* standards; such items functioned as insignia of rank and status (Earle 1987:69–72; Malo 1951:76–77). The exceptional value of red and yellow feather items was due, in part, to the labor and resources required for their manufacture; some *kāhili*, for example, could have incorporated 80,000 feathers from 13,000 birds (Rose et al. 1993:300).

Although barkcloth was often a more mundane clothing material, it too was highly valued in early contact-period Hawaiian society. Barkcloth was manufactured with the inner bark of the paper mulberry tree or other plant fibers (Abbott 1992:50–51). The production of barkcloth was time-consuming and effort was often expended to decorate it with elaborate geometric patterns using various plant-based pigments (Abbott 1992:51–58; Malo 1951:48–50). The rich cultural meaning of barkcloth in traditional Hawaiian society is evidenced by the fact that there was a deity of barkcloth makers, Maikoha (Krauss 1993:60); barkcloth was also used as tribute to elites (Malo 1951:29–30, 78).

The most commonly worn barkcloth garments included a loincloth for males, a skirt for females, and a shawl for members of both genders (Krauss 1993:70–71). The skirt was crafted with wide segments of barkcloth that were wrapped around an elite woman's torso between her bust and knees. Among commoner women, barkcloth skirts covered only the area between her waist and her knees. Generally speaking, the higher a woman's status, the greater the number of barkcloth layers that covered her midriff and thighs (Arthur 1998:272). In the late 1880s, the indigenous Hawaiian historian David Malo noted that the loincloth was used by men "as a covering for the immodest parts" and that the skirt was "wrapped about the loins [and] shielded the modesty of the women" (Malo 1951:78). Thus, it is possible that Hawaiians valued some degree of sexual modesty even before Christian missionaries arrived in 1820.

Due to the equable climate of the islands, protection from the cold was unnecessary for most coastal lowland residents, although barkcloth was used for warmth on cool evenings (Malo 1951:78). At higher elevations, where canoe builders, bird catchers, and stone adze makers worked, warm clothing would have been necessary (Bayman and Moniz-Nakamura 2001:249; Bayman et al. 2004:99–100). From a practical standpoint, clothing was an obvious imperative in traditional Hawaiian society.

In keeping with their religious ideology, however, American missionaries urged Hawaiian women to adopt Western clothing styles, such as the *holokū* (Figure 7.1), because these garments covered women's bodies (Arthur 1998:274–275). Missionaries also tried to conceal women's bodies and sexuality elsewhere in Oceania (Brock 2007; Thomas 2002:183). Sometimes called the "Mother Hubbard," the *holokū* that was brought to Hawai'i was eagerly adopted by elite Hawaiian women to assert their social connections with Americans (Arthur 1998:272–274; Kamehiro 2007). Some Hawaiian queens and chiefesses commissioned missionary wives as seamstresses to satisfy their desire for Western clothing (McClellan 1950; Thurston 1882). In short, elite Hawaiian women authorized the local production of Western-style clothing to visibly convey a nontraditional dimension of their hoped-for affinity with Euro-American society.

While the introduction of Western clothing by American missionaries might be viewed as symptomatic of colonial oppression, elite women used it as a symbol of their power and prestige, since commoner women were initially unable to acquire Western fabric. In this regard, it is notable that

Figure 7.1: Hawaiians in western clothing. Note: The women are wearing holokū.
Unknown photographer, Bishop Museum.

Hawaiian queens compelled the wives of missionaries to provide them with
holokū, in exchange for permission to extend their stay in the islands
(Thurston 1882). According to an American, Lucy Thurston, one queen
also demanded that her *holokū* be altered to accommodate the humid tropical climate of the islands (Thurston 1882:31).

In the 1830s, missionary women taught sewing to common Hawaiian
women who began making *holokū* with barkcloth, rather than imported fabric (Bishop 1887). The adoption of a Western clothing style crafted with traditional materials offers an intriguing instance of technological hybridity. By
1837, the Western *holokū* had largely replaced the traditional skirt and
become standard dress for Hawaiian women (Arthur 1998:276).

Although traditional skirts were apparently still worn by a few Hawaiian
women in 1851, they were exceedingly rare (Andersson 1854:1). This documentary observation was corroborated through a content analysis of photographic archives in the Bishop Museum (Arthur 1998:276). In photographs
that postdate 1859, women were routinely depicted wearing the missionary-
introduced *holokū* (Arthur 1998:276), unless they were posing for a staged
image. Although it is possible that some women still wore traditional Hawaiian barkcloth after 1859, the absence of candid photographic images of such

women implies that *holokū* and other styles of Western clothing were dominant. Of course, Hawaiian women may have still worn barkcloth clothing in remote areas of the islands that photographers did not regularly visit. The persistence of traditional clothing in the interior of central Australia (Brock 2007) offers an example of such behavior in a post-contact society.

In either case, traditional barkcloth garments that were worn by indigenous Hawaiian women were largely replaced with Western garments in no more than 40 years, and perhaps less than 20 years. Among commoners, however, the Western-derived *holokū* was often made with barkcloth, at least until the middle of the nineteenth century. One observer noted that by 1851, traditional barkcloth skirts were "getting rare, like most other things of by-gone days" (Anderson 1854:10). This particular instance of rapid technological change was clearly connected with the power of Christian ideology in the Hawaiians Islands. The efforts of elite women to acquire Western fabrics and clothing exemplify the political machinations that instigated technological change and the construction of dual traditional and Western identities by Hawaiians (cf. Kamehiro 2007). Hawaiian women's rapid adoption of Western clothing styles contrasts sharply with the persistence of some characteristics of traditional architecture.

Vernacular Architecture

Vernacular architecture is distinguished by characteristics that mirror the societies in which it is constructed and used. Generally speaking, vernacular architecture signals an attachment to traditional places, it is used on a daily basis by ordinary people, it is constructed with local building materials, and it has both utilitarian and affective functions (Brunskill 1981:24; Rapoport 1969:4–5; Rensel 1997:10). Architecture "is said to be traditional when its design reflects knowledge exclusive to a local culture and when the economic relationships formed by the need for materials remain within one area" (Coiffier 1988:ix). Vernacular architecture structures daily life by partitioning domestic activities (Hillier and Hanson 1984). By influencing "patterns of encounter and avoidance" (Cameron 1998:187) architecture simultaneously activates and reflects social relations. Architecture is non-portable, it is rarely observed by non-local populations, it often entails capital investment, and it reflects relatively long-term social and economic arrangements. Not surprisingly, vernacular architecture is often quite resistant to rapid change.

In light of these qualities, vernacular architecture in the Hawaiian Islands is amenable to study: it was constructed by a demonstrably indigenous society, it was suited to local environmental conditions, and it sustained cultural values and practices (Rensel 1997:12). Although traditional architecture is commonly imagined to be timeless and unchanging, it is, in fact, characterized by continuous change (Upton and Vlatch 1986). Because Hawaiian archaeologists have just begun to date traditional residential features and have not accumulated much information on change over time (Dye 2010), this discussion considers the century and a half that followed European contact, with the goal of inferring the ideological and sociopolitical dimensions that underlay its persistence and transformation.

Examining this transformation requires information on architecture before contact. Unfortunately, perishable elements of traditional Hawaiian pole-and-thatch *hale* are not preserved in the archaeological record. Thus, information on precontact construction techniques is limited to foundations and floors, stone enclosures, and post molds (e.g., Hommon 1970; Tuggle and Griffin 1973; Weisler and Kirch 1985). However, ethnohistoric accounts and photographs from the late eighteenth and early nineteenth centuries offer relatively detailed insights on the appearance, functions, and development of pole-and-thatch *hale* after contact (e.g., Buck 1957; Brigham 1908; Judd 1975; Peterson 1964; Schmitt 1981). This summary refers to Apple (1971), an exhaustive analysis of Hawaiian vernacular architecture.

At European contact and for several decades afterward, pole-and-thatch *hale* were typically rectangular single-room structures built atop a stone platform and/or within an enclosing stone wall (Figure 7.2). Wooden posts, rafters, and purlins were lashed together with plant fiber cordage to form a hipped or gabled roof. Before contact, doorways were apparently a relatively small opening that could be easily covered with a mat. Once it was lashed together, the pole frame was covered with plant fiber thatch.

Traditionally, pole-and-thatch *hale* were used for storage, shelter, and security (Apple 1971:3). The objects stored in a *hale* depended on its particular use, but could include crafted materials, canoes and fishing gear, and ritual paraphernalia. Climate offered an incentive for using pole-and-thatch *hale*, since temperature extremes in coastal settings, where habitation settlements were concentrated, range in degrees Fahrenheit between the mid-50s and upper 90s. One visitor to Hawai'i in 1837 noted that pole-and-thatch *hale* were cool during warm days and warm on cool evenings (Hinds

Figure 7.2: Homes in ʻOlaʻa, Hawaiʻi. "The New and the Old," circa 1889.
Source: P. L. Lord, Bishop Museum.

1968:116, 117). Similarly, ethnographic and archaeological studies confirm that thermal efficiency is a cross-cultural regularity of vernacular architecture throughout the world (Gilman 1987).

Of particular interest, Apple (1971) notes that pole-and-thatch *hale* offered protection for commoners and lesser elite during times of taboo. The *kapu* system was practiced in traditional Hawaiian society to ensure that the purity of elite *mana* was not polluted by contact with profane objects and/or commoners (Valeri 1985a:90–105). During taboo periods, commoners and other low-ranking individuals avoided being seen or heard by elites (Apple 1971:8–10), because acts as simple as casting one's shadow on the back of a king were punishable by death (Malo 1951:56; Valeri 1985a:91). Periods of taboo included burial processions, sacred temple ceremonies, and other religious events.

To accommodate the need for security and other socially constructed imperatives, *hale* were often grouped together into a household compound. Typically, a compound might include a men's house, a sleeping house for both males and females, and a menstruation house. In some compounds, there were eating houses for women, as well as other *hale* for storage, cooking, and other activities (Handy and Pukui 1972; Malo 1951; Van Gilder 2001). Unlike European houses, the interiors of traditional Hawaiian houses were normally not partitioned into rooms (Campbell 1967:130; Ellis 1979:225; Ledyard 1964:128).

After the traditional Hawaiian religion was terminated by indigenous elites in 1819 (Kuykendall 1938:102), the construction and spatial configuration of *hale* underwent marked changes. For example, doorways into *hale* were enlarged so that crawling was no longer necessary to enter them, and window openings were cut into walls to admit air and light (Apple 1971:200–201). This was a striking departure from the early nineteenth-century enactment of "birth-of-house" ceremonies when the cutting of small doorways symbolically represented the severing of *hale* umbilical cords (Malo 1951:121–125).

Moreover, multi-building compounds were increasingly nucleated after the traditional religion and *kapu* system were overthrown (Ladefoged 1991:57). In other words, *hale* that once would have been separate buildings were integrated as rooms of larger structures. The strictures of the traditional Hawaiian religion were no longer a hindrance to those who wished to organize their households in this Euro-American style, and traditional pole-and-thatch *hale* waned. It was no longer necessary, for example, to ensure that sleeping and cooking were practiced in separate areas.

The architectural innovations that followed the demise of the traditional religion in 1819 were intensified by the arrival of missionaries, who introduced New England–style architecture in 1821 (Sandler et al. 1993:11). When they first settled, frames for missionary houses were fabricated by carpenters in Boston before they were brought to Hawai'i. Shortly thereafter, local building materials, including coral blocks and whitewashed adobe bricks, were often used by missionaries as well as Hawaiians (Judd 1975:61; Sandler et al. 1993:11–12), especially for royal palaces, churches, and other civic buildings (see Mills 1996:205–262). As a consequence, most vestiges of traditional domestic *hale* were abandoned in urban settings by the mid- to late-nineteenth century. Photographs and artistic renditions of Honolulu indicate that pole-and-thatch *hale* were no longer present in downtown Honolulu after 1890 and that they were increasingly rare in rural O'ahu (Apple 1971:216).

Although pole-and-thatch *hale* largely disappeared on O'ahu by the beginning of the twentieth century, some were still present as late as 1920 in isolated coastal settlements on islands such as Moloka'i. However, such houses typically reflected a hybrid blend of Hawaiian and Western architectural styles and materials. For example, many Hawaiian *hale* were built with traditional thatched walls and imported corrugated metal roofs (Apple 1971:201). According to one writer, the last "grass thatcher" died in 1879 (Doyle 1953:206). Another source argues that the craftsmen who built traditional *hale* at Ki'ilae Village, on Hawai'i Island, died in the early 1900s (Jackson and States 1966:51–56). In either case, the use of pole-and-thatch *hale* persisted in isolated areas, albeit in a modified form, until the early twentieth century.

The Archaeology of Emergent Colonialism in Hawai'i

The sources and speed of technological change varied among adzes, clothing styles, and vernacular buildings in post-contact Hawai'i. These materials played different roles in the technological construction of social identity by elites and commoners in the wake of emergent colonialism, and they are differentially preserved in the archaeological record. Unlike stone adzes, which are well documented in the archaeological record of post-contact Hawai'i, residential houses are only marginally preserved and clothing almost never so. Thus, historic documents and photographs are necessary to examine building and clothing styles and technologies. Our review of these materials reveals the following trends: (i) Western *holokū* dresses were adopted by Hawaiian women and replaced traditional barkcloth skirts less than 40 years after their introduction by Christian missionaries; (ii) metal tools replaced stone adzes almost 100 years after their introduction by Europeans; and (iii) pole-and-thatch *hale* persisted in some remote locations for 140 years after European contact, although their configuration and layout changed.

What factors might account for striking differences in the rate with which traditional Hawaiian technologies were modified and eventually replaced with European and American alternatives? This archaeological study indicates that a variety of ideological, political, and economic factors influenced the rate with which different non-traditional technologies were accepted by Hawaiians in the post-contact period. Hawaiian elites were an important influence in all three instances of technological change, along with the introduction of Christian ideologies and a capitalist economy that entailed trade relations with China, Europe, and North America. Moreover, in each case, elite Hawaiians exercised their power to control access to non-local materials and to influence the character of technological change. In so doing, they constructed a hybrid identity that integrated characteristics of both traditional and Western culture. The degree to which particular changes in technology were intentional varied across categories of material culture.

The Hawaiian case exemplifies the way in which "cultural entanglement" (sensu Alexander 1998:485–486) may instigate rapid social and technological change, even before colonialism has fully developed. For example, the relatively rapid adoption of certain styles of Western clothing by Hawaiian women illustrates the influence of Christian missionaries who sought to control the sexuality of native women (see Silva (2000) for a relevant discussion). It is noteworthy, however, that elite Hawaiian women eagerly commissioned the production of *holokū* because such garments visibly materialized their relationships with immigrant American missionaries. This effort by elite women to convey their connection with American missionary society is a dramatic example of how hybrid identities were technologically and socially constructed in emergent colonial settings. Common women, who initially had no access to imported fabric, made their *holokū* out of barkcloth, a traditional medium for clothing. Barkcloth production was an exceptionally labor-intensive undertaking, but its manufacture only required locally available materials, in contrast with the fabric imported from the United States, Europe, and China.

The adoption of metal tools was slower than the adoption of the *holokū*. Although Hawaiians eagerly sought metal after contact with Europeans and then Americans, access to it by commoners was initially constrained by elite prerogative. Even though elite control of metal adzes in the early post-contact period did not necessarily materialize their hybrid identity (sensu Bhabha 1994) as strongly as did Western clothing, it did reflect the impact of indigenous social stratification on technological change (sensu Pfaffenberger 1992). When Hawaiian chiefs developed an insatiable desire for sandalwood some 50 years after contact, their interest in mobilizing large amounts of it through tribute encouraged them to facilitate commoner access to metal tools. Commoners with metal tools could gather sandalwood much more quickly than commoners with stone adzes, so it was in the best interests of the elite to allow wider access to metal.

In contrast, the persistence of pole-and-thatch *hale* for more than a century after contact can be partially explained by their desirable "performance characteristics" in a sub-tropical climate. Pole-and-thatch buildings offered a cost-effective source of shelter that was easily constructed with locally available materials. Temperature control was one of their greatest assets in Hawai'i. Although pole-and-thatch *hale* persisted far longer than many other traditional technologies, certain facets of architecture did change in the face of European and American contact. As noted earlier, the arrangement of functionally particular *hale* was no longer desirable or necessary following termination of the traditional Hawaiian religion, which required the separation of sacred and profane activities. Hawaiian conversion to Christianity nullified a major design imperative of their houses: the strict spatial separation of cooking, sleeping, menstruation, and other activities was no longer necessary.

Change in architecture, like change in adzes and clothing, was initially driven by elites, who were among the first converts to Christianity. The simultaneous use of both traditional houses and Western-style buildings by some elites (see Mills 1996:205–262) offers yet another example of how technology embodied their indigenous and Western identities.

Conclusions

Historical events in nineteenth-century Hawai'i exemplify the idea that "culture contact is structured, but its outcomes are not determined" (Alexander 1998:477). In this respect, the archaeological record offers an exceptional opportunity to study the complex sources of technological change before and after contact and colonialism. Examples set out in this chapter confirm that technological change was due to several influences and that it varied among materials in post-contact Hawai'i, including adzes, clothing, and vernacular architecture.

In Hawai'i, material culture played an important role in the creation and maintenance of hybrid identities, especially among indigenous elites. Of course, Euro-Americans who resided in Hawai'i also constructed hybrid identities—behavior that is beyond the scope of this chapter. Elite prerogatives, Christianity, international capitalism, and many other factors instigated rapid change in female clothing fashions. In contrast, the persistence of traditional stone adzes and pole-and-thatch *hale* for more than a century illustrates the impact of other economic and political factors in delaying the seemingly inevitable onset of technological change after contact. This study confirms that the rate of technological change in Hawai'i was heavily influenced by the kings, queens, and chiefs who ruled their subjects. The Hawaiian example confirms that technological change and social identity were multi-dimensional and that more nuanced analyses must be undertaken to understand them in the world of the Pacific islands.

8

Reconciling Archaeology and History

As we noted in Chapter 1, the overthrow and annexation of the Kingdom of Hawai'i by the United States of America in the late nineteenth century was followed by the arrival of Hawaii's first archaeologist, and now more than a century of scholarly research. Our review of the archaeology of contact and colonialism in Chapter 7 does not consider the profound consequences of the overthrow for archaeology today. This chapter chronicles, albeit briefly, the ramifications of the overthrow for contemporary archaeology and society in the islands. Native Hawaiians have been engaged in a struggle to define and implement a vision for restoring their sociopolitical self-determination, and their efforts are changing the practice of archaeology in the islands.

To some native Hawaiians, the overthrow was part of a larger effort by the United States to control the islands for their strategic value in the emerging geopolitical arena of the early twentieth century. Shortly after the overthrow, Queen Lili'uokalani was held under house arrest in 'Iolani Palace. During her incarceration, the islands were ruled by an insurgent Provisional Government that was administrated by non-Hawaiians. Little more than a year later, the so-called "Republic of Hawai'i" was established. Four years later the United States Congress passed a joint resolution and the short-lived "republic" was annexed as a U.S. Territory in 1898. Finally, in 1959, Hawai'i became the fiftieth state.

Many citizens of the United States are well aware that Hawai'i is one of only two states, along with Alaska, that are not part of the continental United States. Relatively few U.S. citizens, however, seem to know much, if anything, about the history of the "occupied" Hawaiian Islands. Popular images of Hawai'i bear witness to the conventional idea that it is a tropical paradise, a place to vacation and enjoy the warm climate and blue waters of the Pacific Ocean. Relatively few citizens of the continental United States are aware of the deep and lingering bitterness that some Hawaiians feel about the historical circumstances that have left many of them without land, and all of them without indigenous self-determination. To this day, there is not a widely recognized government for indigenous Hawaiians, and this fact complicates the practice of archaeology in the islands.

Hawaiian Land and Identity

Problems stemming from the legacy of the overthrow regularly confront archaeologists who practice in Hawai'i. Ironically, some of these archaeologists are themselves native Hawaiians. The "archaeological record" of dispassionate scholarship is the earthly embodiment of native Hawaiian ancestry and identity. In Hawaiian epistemology, cultural identity stems from genealogical connection to the taro plant that grew from the buried stillborn child of the Hawaiian progenitor gods, Papa and Wākea. Because Hawaiian identity is established through this vital connection to the land, Hawaiians have a somatic attachment to the islands. In the traditional Hawaiian worldview, their identity through land legitimizes their place on the land.

Archaeology—almost by definition—is the study of people, their history, and their land throughout the world. Yet, the lands studied by archaeologists are typically empty of living Hawaiians. Over the past two centuries, indigenous Hawaiians have lost much of the land that was once cared for by their ancestors. In 1848, several decades before the illegal overthrow of the kingdom, the *Māhele*, which introduced private ownership of land, was institutionalized by King Kamehameha III. Kamehameha acted in the face of threats to Hawaiian sovereignty, and with encouragement from some of his non-Hawaiian advisors, to institute a landholding regime that would survive conquest by a foreign power (Banner 2005). Privy Council records show that he believed this was the best way to ensure that Hawai'i remained Hawaiian land. Initially, lands were awarded in fee simple, subject to the rights of native tenants. This process resulted in the king keeping 2.5 million acres, of which he ceded 1.5 million acres to the government, in awards of 1.6 million acres to 240 chiefs, and in 28,658 acres being divided among 8,421 commoners at a time when the population was roughly 72,000 (Linnekin 1987:27). This was followed over the next decades by the sale of government lands to individual Hawaiians, whereby another 167,000 acres was transferred to Hawaiian commoners (Preza 2010). In the early years of the new system, commoners who chose not to apply for fee-simple awards saw their rights as native tenants respected, and they continued to gain access to land in the traditional ways (Chinen 2002; Lam 1989). In 1858, however, an activist Supreme Court handed down a decision authored by a native Scotsman without legal training that proscribed many of these traditional access rights (Van Dyke 2008:83). Thus, the process of land tenure reform was accomplished in Hawai'i by a forward-looking native Hawaiian government whose desire to protect the rights of native tenants was thwarted, in part, by an activist Supreme Court.

This land reform instigated the alienation of land in the non-traditional "free market" economy of world capitalism. Land that was once held in trust by Hawaiian rulers, on behalf of themselves and their subjects, was no longer shared in the traditional manner. The *Māhele*, and later the overthrow and annexation of the kingdom itself, sped the transfer of land from indigenous Hawaiians to non-Hawaiians, many of them with American citizenship. This transfer of traditional lands had far-reaching effects on Hawaiian economy and society. Families of Hawaiian farmers, for example, were suddenly dependent on non-Hawaiians for access to productive agricultural land. Moreover, the transfer of land undermined the traditional view of Hawaiian identity.

Hawaiian Views of Archaeology

Many Hawaiians have mixed but often negative views of archaeology (Kawelu 2007). In Hawai'i, this view of archaeology portends the modification of land and the desecration of its ancient burials and sacred cultural sites. Indeed, archaeology in Hawai'i is most often featured in the local news when human skeletal remains are encountered through real estate development. International tourism since statehood has accelerated the construction of hotels, golf courses, roads, and local workforce housing, schools, and shopping centers. Since 9/11 and the "War on Terror," Hawai'i has witnessed an expansion of the US military on its islands. In the eyes of many Hawaiians as well as non-Hawaiians, the increased presence of the US military endangers sacred cultural sites and burials.

Although the disturbance of most cultural sites is typically troubling to Hawaiians, there is a special concern with the treatment of human remains.

Many Hawaiians believe that human remains should remain undisturbed. Unfortunately, however, human remains in unmarked graves are routinely encountered, often inadvertently, during economic development, despite the widespread agreement among Hawaiians that mortuary sites should be avoided. Often, human remains discovered in the process of land development are disinterred by archaeologists after decisions on their treatment have been made by one of the Island Burial Councils or by the State Historic Preservation Division, typically in consultation with a burial council.

Each major island in the archipelago has a council of Hawaiians and non-Hawaiians that plays a role in determining how human remains in unmarked graves are to be treated upon their discovery. The Island Burial Councils have largely proven successful in restoring the ability of native Hawaiians to take care of ancestral burials on lands alienated since the *Māhele*. Their volunteer members provide a tremendous public service. However, the work of the councils is complicated by Hawaii's high land values, which put a premium on development, and the often intense politics that accompany this situation.

An example is an ongoing dispute over the removal of native Hawaiian remains from the grounds of Kawaiaha'o Church, the so-called Westminster Abbey of Hawai'i. The church, which has a predominantly native Hawaiian congregation and is led by a native Hawaiian minister, is planning to build a revenue-generating facility on a previously developed portion of its property that a land survey indicates was once part of the cemetery adjoining the church. The Hawai'i law that created the Island Burial Councils was written to extend the protections afforded cemetery burials to the unmarked, mostly native Hawaiian, burials discovered or located outside of registered cemeteries. That law recognizes the exigencies of development and in certain circumstances bypasses the Island Burial Councils and gives state government authority to determine burial treatment on a fast track.

Many native Hawaiians and others were indignant when archaeologists hired by the church and sanctioned by the state under this law removed more than 70 coffin burials from the cemetery, classifying them as "inadvertent discoveries." Construction of the facility was held up for more than a year while two lawsuits brought by native Hawaiians were resolved. (Disclosure: two of us—TSD and EKK—were hired by the plaintiff in one of these lawsuits). A third lawsuit, also brought by a native Hawaiian, is making its way through the court at the time of this writing. Construction of the facility recently resumed, along with the removal of coffin burials, sparking organized protests outside the church during and after Sunday morning services. These protests principally target the church congregation, but are also critical of the archaeologists who dig up graves from burial plots associated with living families.

The repatriation of sacred items from museums and other public and private institutions is another vexing issue facing indigenous Hawaiians, archaeologists, and other ethnic communities in Hawai'i. In one repatriation dispute, a Hawaiian man was imprisoned for three weeks for refusing to tell a federal judge where his group had reburied artifacts from Bishop Museum that officials there contended were on loan. The artifacts in question were removed from a cave with burials about a century ago and were housed in Bishop Museum for many years. Although deliberations among thirteen or so claimants and the court system are still underway, the outcome of this particular dispute will likely remain unresolved for some time. The claimants include members of several indigenous families and cultural organizations who have different visions of how the artifacts in question should be treated.

Reconciling Archaeology and History in Hawai'i

Relations between native Hawaiians and archaeologists might have reached their nadir in the 1980s and 1990s; the relationship seems to be improving since then (Kawelu 2007). This improvement is likely due to the increasing involvement of native Hawaiians in historic preservation. Highly visible manifestations of this trend are the reconstructed temples at the shoreline in Kahalu'u on Hawai'i Island (Figure 8.1). These two temples, which were in ruins a few years ago, are being rebuilt by native Hawaiians with a plan for their adaptive reuse and re-dedication in 2014. The regular activities of the Island Burial Councils also play a major role. Here, archaeologists are typically involved as technical specialists and not in decision-making roles. This has given many native Hawaiians a chance to learn what archaeology can and cannot accomplish. The last two decades have seen an expanding presence of native Hawaiians in the field, as cultural monitors, fieldworkers, and increasingly as archaeologists trained at mainland universities or in new and expanding programs at the University of Hawai'i. Last, but certainly not least, has been the leadership role assumed by native Hawaiians lobbying for

Figure 8.1: Hāpaialiʻi and Keʻekū Heiau, two temples recently reconstructed by a subsidiary of Kamehameha Schools, the legacy of the Kamehameha Dynasty.

more effective historic preservation laws and their conscientious application (Cachola-Abad and Ayau 1999).

The interests of native Hawaiians participating in historic preservation today often diverge and it would be wrong to speak of a unified view of archaeology among them. In comparison to non-native archaeologists, however, their interests are often place-based and intensely historical, rather than regional and processual. In practice, this difference often plays out as a distinction between insider and outsider views of Hawaiʻi and its native culture. Native Hawaiians typically bring a full respect for tradition, not as a passive record of history, but as "a type of historical truth that is culture specific ... that explains the how and why of present day conditions" (Kikiloi 2010:109, n. 4). In this way, archaeology is contributing to efforts by a younger generation of scholars to decolonize their thinking and connect more directly with the past of their ancestors, while they lead Hawaiian archaeology in new directions.

Hawaiian Terms

ahupua'a Traditional Hawaiian land division, usually extending from the uplands to the sea.

hale House, building, station, hall.

heiau Traditional Hawaiian place of worship.

hōlua Sled, especially the ancient sled used on grassy slopes; the sled course.

'ili A land section, next in importance to *ahupua'a*, and usually a subdivision of an *ahupua'a*.

kapu Taboo, prohibition; special privilege or exemption from ordinary taboo; sacredness; prohibited, forbidden; sacred, holy, consecrated; no trespassing, keep out.

kī A woody shrub, *Cordyline terminalis*, in the lily family. Traditionally, the leaves were used for a variety of purposes, such as wearing apparel, thatching, food, fishing, and religious purposes. The root was eaten in times of famine and was the basis in historic times for *'ōkolehao*, a fermented drink.

kou A native tree, *Cordia subcordata*, with a wood prized for its grain and ease of carving. It was used for carving a wide variety of objects from platters to images of gods; the leaves were made into dye and the flowers were also used in *lei* making.

kuaiwi Long, straight stone wall.

kukui The candlenut tree, *Aleurites moluccana*, introduced to Hawai'i by Polynesian settlers. The outer husk of the fruit or nut was used to make a black dye for tapa and tattooing; sap from the fruit was used as medicine to treat thrush, and used as a purgative; the hard shell of the nut was used in *lei* making; the kernel of the nut was the source of an oil that was burned for illumination and also used as a wood varnish for surfboards and canoes; the kernel was also chewed and spit on rough seas to calm the ocean, and baked kernels were mixed with salt and chili pepper to make a relish (*'inamona*); the trunk was used to make canoes and floats for fishing nets; a reddish dye was made from the bark and/or root; a gum exuded from wounded bark was used to treat tapa; the flower was mixed with sweet potato to treat thrush; the leaves were used in a poultice for swelling and infection.

lei Garland, wreath.

luakini *Heiau* of the ruling chiefs where human sacrifices were offered. See also *heiau*.

Māhele The mid-nineteenth century land division responsible for the introduction of fee simple land title in Hawai'i.

makahiki Ancient festival beginning about the middle of October and lasting about four months, with sports and religious festivities and a taboo on war.

makai Seaward.

mana Supernatural or divine power, mana, miraculous power.

mauka Inland, upland, toward the mountain.

Menehune Legendary race of small people who worked at night, building fish ponds, roads, temples; if the work was not finished in one night, it remained unfinished.

milo A tree or arborescent shrub, Thespesia populnea, either indigenous or introduced by Polynesians for its wood and fiber.

moa Chicken, red jungle chicken (*Gallus gallus*), fowl, as brought to Hawai'i by Polynesians.

moku District, island, section; forest, grove.

pāhoehoe Basaltic lava flows typified by smooth, billowy, or ropy surface.

poi The Hawaiian staff of life, made from cooked taro corms, or, rarely, breadfruit, pounded and thinned with water.

References

Abbott, Isabella A.
1992 *Lāʻau Hawaiʻi: Traditional Hawaiian Uses of Plants*. Bishop Museum Press, Honolulu.

Alexander, R. T.
1998 Afterword: Toward an Archaeological Theory of Culture Contact. In *Studies in Culture Contact: Interaction, Culture Change, and Archaeology*, edited by James G. Cusick, pp. 476–495. Occasional Papers 25. Center for Archaeological Investigations, Southern Illinois University, Carbondale.

Allen, Jane (editor)
1987 *Five Upland ʻIli: Archaeological and Historical Investigations in the Kaneʻohe Interchange, Interstate Highway H-3, Island of Oʻahu*. Departmental Report Series 87–1. Anthropology Department, B. P. Bishop Museum, Honolulu.
1991 The Role of Agriculture in the Evolution of the Pre-Contact Hawaiian State. *Asian Perspectives* 30(1):117–132.

Allen, Jane, Mary R. Riford, Paul Brennan, David Chaffee, Linda Scott Cummings, Carol Kawachi, Laurie Liu, and Gail Murakami
2002 *Kula and Kahawai: Geoarchaeological and Historic Investigations in Middle Maunawili Valley, Kailua, Koʻolau Poko, Oʻahu*. AMEC Earth and Environmental, Honolulu. Submitted to HRT, Ltd.

Allen, Melinda S.
1996 Style and Function in East Polynesian Fish-Hooks. *Antiquity* 70:97–116.
2001 The Kona Field System in Spatial and Temporal Perspective. In *Gardens of Lono: Archaeological Investigations at the Amy B. H. Greenwell Ethnobotanical Garden, Kealakekua, Hawaiʻi*, edited by Melinda S. Allen, Chapter 11:137–155. Bishop Museum Press, Honolulu.
2004 Bet-Hedging Strategies, Agricultural Change, and Unpredictable Environments: Historical Development of Dryland Agriculture in Kona, Hawaii. *Journal of Anthropological Archaeology* 23:196–224.

Allen, Melinda S. (editor)
2001 *Gardens of Lono: Archaeological Investigations at the Amy B. H. Greenwell Ethnobotanical Garden, Kealakekua, Hawaiʻi*. Bishop Museum Press, Honolulu.

Allen, Melinda S. and Patricia A. McAnany
  1994 Environmental Variability and Traditional Hawaiian Land Use Patterns: Manukā's Cultural Islands in Seas of Lava. *Asian Perspectives* 33(1):19–55.
Allen, Melinda S. and Gail Murakami
  1999 Lana'i Island's Arid Lowland Vegetation in Late Prehistory. *Pacific Science* 53:88–112.
Álvaro Montenegro, Chris Avis, and Andrew Weaver
  2008 Modeling the Prehistoric Arrival of Sweet Potato in Polynesia. *Journal of Archaeological Science* 35:355–367.
Ames, Kenneth M.
  1995 Chiefly Power and Household Production on the Northwest Coast. In *Foundations of Inequality*, edited by T. Douglas Price and Gary M. Feinman, pp. 155–188. Plenum Press, New York.
Anderson, Atholl
  1989 *Prodigious Birds: Moas and Moa-Hunting in Prehistoric New Zealand.* Cambridge University Press, Cambridge and New York.
Anderson, Atholl and Yosihiko H. Sinoto
  2002 New Radiocarbon Ages of Colonization Sites in East Polynesia. *Asian Perspectives* 41(2):242–257.
Andersson, Nils
  1854 *A Voyage Around the World with the Swedish Frigate Eugenie.* J. B. Wolters, Gröningen.
Andrade, Carlos
  2008 *Hā'ena: Through the Eyes of the Ancestors.* University of Hawai'i Press, Honolulu.
Apple, Russell A.
  1971 *Hawaiian Thatched House: Use—Construction—Adaptation.* National Park Service, San Francisco.
Arkush, Elizabeth N. and Mark D. Allen (editors)
  2006 *The Archaeology of Warfare: Prehistories of Raiding and Conquest.* University of Florida Press, Gainesville, Florida.
Arthur, Linda B.
  1998 Hawaiian Women and Dress: The *Holokū* as an Expression of Ethnicity. *Fashion Theory* 2:269–286.
  1999 *Religion, Dress, and the Body.* Berg, Oxford and New York.
Athens, J. Stephen
  1997 Hawaiian Native Lowland Vegetation in Prehistory. In *Historical Ecology in the Pacific Islands: Prehistoric Environmental and Landscape Change*, edited by Patrick V. Kirch and Terry L. Hunt, Chapter 12:248–270. Yale University Press, New Haven, Connecticut.
  2008 *Rattus exulans* and the Catastrophic Disappearance of Hawai'i's Native Lowland Forest. *Biological Invasions.*

Athens, J. Stephen (editor)
2000 *Ancient Hawaiian Fishponds of Pearl Harbor: Archaeological Studies on U.S. Navy Lands, Hawai'i.* International Archaeological Research Institute, Honolulu. Submitted to State Historic Preservation Division, Department of Land and Natural Resources. Department of Defense Legacy Resource Management Program, Project No. 1729.

Athens, J. Stephen, Michael W. Kaschko, and Helen F. James
1991 Prehistoric Bird Hunters: High Altitude Resource Exploitation on Hawai'i Island. *Bishop Museum Occasional Papers* 31:63–84.

Athens, J. Stephen, Jerome V. Ward, H. David Tuggle, and David J. Welch
1999 *Environment, Vegetation Change, and Early Human Settlement on the 'Ewa Plain: A Cultural Resource Inventory of Naval Air Station, Barbers Point, O'ahu, Hawai'i, Part III: Paleoenvironmental Investigations.* International Archaeological Research Institute, Honolulu. Submitted to Department of the Navy.

Athens, J. Stephen, H. David Tuggle, Jerome V. Ward, and David J. Welch
2002 Avifaunal Extinctions, Vegetation Change, and Polynesian Impacts in Prehistoric Hawai'i. *Archaeology in Oceania* 37:57–78.

Banner, Stuart
2005 Preparing to be Colonized: Land Tenure and Legal Strategy in Nineteenth-Century Hawaii. *Law & Society Review* 39(2):273–314.

Barber, Elizabeth J. W.
1994 *Women's Work, the First 20,000 Years: Women, Cloth, and Society in Early Times.* 1st ed. Norton, New York.

Barrera Jr., William and Patrick V. Kirch
1973 Basaltic Glass Artefacts from Hawaii: Their Dating and Prehistoric Uses. *Journal of the Polynesian Society* 82:176–187.

Bayman, James M.
2003 Stone Adze Economies in Post-Contact Hawai'i. In *Stone Tool Traditions in the Contact Era*, edited by Charles R. Cobb, 94–108. The University of Alabama Press, Tuscaloosa, Alabama.
2008 Technological Change and the Archaeology of Emergent Colonialism in the Kingdom of Hawaii. *International Journal of Historical Archaeology* 13:127–157.
2010 The Precarious "Middle Ground": Exchange and the Reconfiguration of Social Identity in the Hawaiian Kingdom. In *Trade and Exchange: Archaeological Studies from History and Prehistory*, edited by C. D. Dillian and C. L. White, pp. 129–148. Springer, New York.

Bayman, James M. and Jadelyn J. Moniz-Nakamura
2001 Craft Specialization and Adze Production on Hawai'i Island. *Journal of Field Archaeology* 28:239–252.

Bayman, James M., Jadelyn J. Moniz-Nakamura, Timothy M. Rieth, and C. Kanani Paraso
2004 Stone Adze Production and Resource Extraction at Pōhakuloa, Hawai'i Island. *Hawaiian Archaeology* 9:83–104.

Beaglehole, John C. (editor)
1967 *The Journals of Captain James Cook on his Voyages of Discovery. The Voyage of the Resolution and Discovery, 1776–1780*. Vol. 3. Cambridge University Press, for the Hakluyt Society, Cambridge.

Beckwith, Martha W. (editor)
2007 *Kepelino's Traditions of Hawaii*. Revised. Bulletin 95. Originally printed in 1932. Bishop Museum Press, Honolulu.

Bell, Edward
1929 Log of the Chatham. *Honolulu Mercury* 1(4):80–82, 87–90.

Bennett, Wendell C.
1931 *Archaeology of Kauai*. B. P. Bishop Museum Bulletin 80. Bishop Museum Press, Honolulu.

Bhabha, Homi K.
1994 *The Location of Culture*. Routledge, London and New York.

Bishop, Sereno
1887 Jubilee Celebration 1837–1887. The Forbes Notes. Mission Houses Museum, Honolulu.

Bloxam, Andrew
1925 *Diary of Andrew Bloxam*. B. P. Bishop Museum Special Publication 10. Bishop Museum Press, Honolulu.

Bowman, Sheridan
1990 *Radiocarbon Dating*. Interpreting the Past. University of California Press, Berkeley.

Brigham, William T.
1899 *Hawaiian Feather Work*. Vol. 1. Memoirs of the B.P. Bishop Museum 1. Bishop Museum Press, Honolulu.
1902 *Stone Implements of the Ancient Hawaiians*. Vol. 1. Memoirs of the B.P. Bishop Museum 4. Bishop Museum Press, Honolulu.
1906a *Mat and Basket Weaving of the Ancient Hawaiians*. Vol. 1. Memoirs of the B. P. Bishop Museum 4. Bishop Museum Press, Honolulu.
1906b *Old Hawaiian Carvings*. Vol. 2. Memoirs of the B. P. Bishop Museum 2. Bishop Museum Press, Honolulu.
1908 *The Ancient Hawaiian House*. Bishop Museum Press, Honolulu.
1911 *Ka Hana Kapa–The Making of Bark-Cloth in Hawaii*. Vol. 3. Memoirs of the B. P. Bishop Museum. Bishop Museum Press, Honolulu.

Brock, P.
2007 Nakedness and Clothing in Early Encounters Between Aboriginal People of Central Australia, Missionaries, and Anthropologists. *Journal of Colonialism and Colonial History* 8:1–23.

Brumfiel, Elizabeth M. and Timothy K. Earle (editors)
1987 *Specialization, Exchange, and Complex Societies*. Cambridge University Press, Cambridge and New York.

Brunskill, R. W.
1981 *Traditional Buildings of Britain: An Introduction to Vernacular Architecture.* Gollancz in association with P. Crawley, London.

Buck, Caitlin E., William G. Cavanagh, and Clifford D. Litton
1996 *Bayesian Approach to Interpreting Archaeological Data.* Statistics in Practice. John Wiley & Sons, Chichester, United Kingdom.

Buck, Caitlin E., J. Andrés Christen, and Gary James
1999 *BCal: an On-Line Bayesian Radiocarbon Calibration Tool.* http://bcal.sheffield.ac.uk.

Buck, Peter H.
1943 Hawaiian Shark-Tooth Implements. In *Report of the Director for 1942*, B. P. Bishop Museum Bulletin 180, pp. 27–41. Bishop Museum Press, Honolulu.
1944 The Local Evolution of Hawaiian Feather Capes and Cloaks. *Journal of the Polynesian Society* 53:1–16.
1957 *Arts and Crafts of Hawaii.* B. P. Bishop Museum Special Publication 45. Bishop Museum Press, Honolulu.
1959 *Vikings of the Pacific.* Phoenix Books, P31. University of Chicago Press, Chicago.

Buck, Peter H., Kenneth P. Emory, H. D. Skinner, and John F. G. Stokes
1930 Terminology for Ground Stone Cutting-Implements in Polynesia. *Journal of the Polynesian Society* 39(2):174–180.

Burney, David A., Helen F. James, Lida Pigott Burney, Storrs L. Olson, William Kikuchi, Warren L. Wagner, Mara Burney, Deirdre McCloskey, Delores Kikuchi, Frederick V. Grady, Reginald Gage II, and Robert Nishek
2001 Fossil Evidence for a Diverse Biota from Kaua'i and Its Transformation since Human Arrival. *Ecological Monographs* 71(4):615–641.

Burtchard, Greg C.
1996 *Population and Land-Use on the Keauhou Coast. The Mauka Land Inventory Survey, Keauhou, North Kona, Hawai'i Island. Part I: Narrative.* International Archaeological Research Institute, Honolulu. Submitted to Kamehameha Investment Corporation.

Burtchard, Greg C., Bruce A. Jones, and Rey F. Quebral
1996 *Population and Land-Use on the Keauhou Coast. The Mauka Land Inventory Survey, Keauhou, North Kona, Hawai'i Island. Part II: Site Data.* International Archaeological Research Institute, Honolulu. Submitted to Kamehameha Investment Corporation.

Burtchard, Greg C. and Myra J. Tomonari-Tuggle
2004 Agriculture on Leeward Hawai'i Island: The Waimea Agricultural System Reconsidered. *Hawaiian Archaeology* 9:50–73.

Byron, George Anson
1826 *Voyage of H.M.S. Blonde to the Sandwich Islands, in the Years 1824–1825. Captain the Right Hon. Lord Byron, Commander.* J. Murray, London.

Cachola-Abad, C. Kēhaunani and Edward Halealoha Ayau
1999 *He Pane Ho'omalamalama*: Setting the Record Straight and a Second Call for Partnership. *Hawaiian Archaeology* 7:73–82.

Calugay, Cyril and Windy K. McElroy
2005 An Analysis of Coral, Basalt, and Sea Urchin Spine Abrading Tools from Nu'alolo Kai, Kaua'i. In *Na Mea Kahiko o Kaua'i: Archaeological Studies in Kaua'i*, edited by Mike T. Carson and Michael W. Graves, pp. 212–235. Special Publication 2. Society for Hawaiian Archaeology, Honolulu.

Cameron, Catherine
1998 Coursed Adobe Architecture, Style, and Social Boundaries in the American Southwest. In *The Archaeology of Social Boundaries*, edited by Miriam Stark, pp. 183–207. Smithsonian Institution Press, Washington, DC.

Campbell, Archibald
1967 *A Voyage round the World, from 1806 to 1812 in which Japan, Kamschatka, the Aleutian Islands, and the Sandwich Islands were Visited Including a Narrative of the Author's Shipwreck on the Island of Sannack, and his Subsequent Wreck in the Ship's Long-Boat; with an Account of the Present State of the Sandwich Islands, and a Vocabulary of their Language*. University of Hawaii Press for Friends of the Library of Hawaii, Honolulu.

Carneiro, Robert L.
1970 A Theory of the Origin of the State. *Science* 169:733–738.

Carson, Mike T. and Michael W. Graves (editors)
2005 *Na Mea Kahiko o Kaua'i: Archaeological Studies in Kaua'i*. Special Publication 2. Society for Hawaiian Archaeology, Honolulu.

Carter, Laura A.
1990 Protohistoric Material Correlates in Hawaiian Archaeology, AD 1778–1820. MA thesis. University of Hawai'i, Honolulu.

Chatan, R.
2003 The Governor's *Vale Levu*: Architecture and Hybridity at Nasova House, Levuka, Fiji Island. *International Journal of Historical Archaeology* 7:267–292.

Chauvin, Michael E.
2000 Useful and Conceptual Astronomy in Ancient Hawaii. In *Astronomy across Cultures: The History of Non-Western Astronomy*, edited by Helaine Selin, pp. 91–125. Science across Cultures 1. Kluwer Academic Publishers, Dordrecht, Netherlands.

Cheever, Henry T.
1851 *The Island World of the Pacific*. Harpers and Brothers, New York.

Chinen, Jon J.
2002 *They Cried for Help: The Hawaiian Land Revolution of the 1840s and 1850s*. Jon J. Chinen, N.p. Distributed by Xlibris Corp.

Chiu, Min-yung
2004 Fish Remains from Site 4853–1 at Bellows Beach, Waimanalo, O'ahu, Hawaiian Islands. *New Zealand Journal of Archaeology* 24(2002):61–76.

Clarke, Andrew C., Michael K. Burtenshaw, Patricia A. McLenachan, David L. Erickson, and David Penny
 2006 Reconstructing the Origins and Dispersal of the Polynesian Bottle Gourd *(Lagenaria siceraria)*. *Molecular Biology and Evolution* 23(5):893–900.
Cleghorn, Paul L.
 1982 The Mauna Kea Adze Quarry: Technological Analysis and Experimental Results. Ph.D. thesis. University of Hawaiʻi, Honolulu.
 1984 An Historical Review of Polynesian Stone Adze Studies. *Journal of the Polynesian Society* 93:399–421.
 1986 Organizational Structure at the Mauna Kea Adze Quarry Complex, Hawaiʻi. *Journal of Archaeological Science* 13:375–387.
 1992 A Hawaiian Adze Sequence or Just Different Kinds of Adzes? *New Zealand Journal of Archaeology* 14:129–149.
Cleghorn, Paul L., Thomas S. Dye, Marshall I. Weisler, and John Sinton
 1985 A Preliminary Petrographic Study of Hawaiian Stone Adze Quarries. *Journal of the Polynesian Society* 94:235–251.
Cobb, Charles R.
 2003 Introduction: Framing Stone Tool Traditions after Contact. In *Stone Tool Traditions in the Contact Era*, edited by Charles R. Cobb. The University of Alabama Press, Tuscaloosa.
Cobb, John N.
 1903 The Commercial Fisheries of the Hawaiian Islands. *Bulletin of the U.S. Fish Commission* 23(2):717–765.
Coiffier, Christian
 1988 *Traditional Architecture in Vanuatu*. Institute of Pacific Studies, [Suva, Fiji].
Collerson, Kenneth D. and Marshall I. Weisler
 2007 Stone Adze Compositions and the Extent of Ancient Polynesian Voyaging and Trade. *Science* 317:1907–1911.
Collins, Sara L.
 1995 Avifaunal Remains from the Kawailoa Site, Oʻahu Island (BPBM Site 50-Oa-D6-62). *Hawaiian Archaeology* 4:4–16.
Cordy, Ross H.
 1981 *A Study of Prehistoric Social Change: The Development of Complex Societies in the Hawaiian Islands*. Academic Press, New York.
 2000 *Exalted Sits the Chief: The Ancient History of Hawaiʻi Island*. Mutual, Honolulu.
 2004 Considering Archaeological Indicators of the Rise of Appointed Chiefs and the Feudal-Land System in the Hawaiian Islands. *Hawaiian Archaeology* 9:1–24.
Cordy, Ross H. and Michael W. Kaschko
 1980 Prehistoric Archaeology in the Hawaiian Islands: Land Units Associated with Social Groups. *Journal of Field Archaeology* 7:403–416.

Cordy, Ross H., Joseph Tainter, Robert Renger, and Robert Hitchcock
1991 *An Ahupua'a Study: The 1971 Archaeological Work at Kaloko Ahupua'a, North Kona, Hawai'i: Archaeology at Kaloko-Honokōhau National Historical Park.* Western Archeological and Conservation Center Publications in Anthropology 58. National Park Service, U.S. Department of the Interior, Honolulu.

Costin, Cathy L.
1991 Craft Specialization: Issues in Defining, Documenting, and Explaining the Organization of Production. In *Archaeological Method and Theory*, edited by Michael B. Schiffer, pp. 1–56. Vol. 3. University of Arizona, Tucson.

Costin, Cathy L. and Rita P. Wright (editors)
1998 *Craft and Social Identity.* Archaeological Papers of the American Anthropological Association 8. American Anthropological Association, Arlington, Virginia.

Dalton, O. M.
1897 *Notes on an Ethnographical Collection from the West Coast of North America (more Especially California), Hawaii & Tahiti, Formed During the Voyage of Captain Vancouver, 1790-1795, and Now in the British Museum.*

Davis, Bertell D.
1989 *Subsurface Archaeological Reconnaissance Survey and Historical Research at Fort DeRussy, Waikiki, Island of O'ahu, Hawai'i.* International Archaeological Research Institute, Honolulu. Submitted to U.S. Army Engineer District, Pacific Ocean Division.

Daws, Gavan
2006 *Honolulu: The First Century, the Story of the Town to 1876.* Mutual Publishing, Honolulu.

Deagan, K. A.
1988 Neither History nor Prehistory: The Questions that Count in Historical Archaeology. *Historical Archaeology* 22:7–12.

Dickey, Lyle A.
1928 *String Figures from Hawaii.* Bernice P. Bishop Museum Bulletin 54. Bishop Museum Press, Honolulu.

Dixon, Boyd and Maurice Major
2011 Floodwater Farming of Ritual Offerings at Kaunolū and Māmaki on Leeward Lāna'i, Hawai'i. *Hawaiian Archaeology* 12:27–46.

Dixon, Boyd, Patty J. Conte, Valerie Nagahara, and W. Koa Hodgins
2002 Settlement Patterns and Subsistence Strategies in Kahikinui, Maui. *Hawaiian Archaeology* 8:13–32.

Dockall, John
2000 *Use, Maintenance, and Discard of Basalt Adzes: A Case Study from Anahulu Valley.* Paper presented at the 13th Annual Conference of the Society for Hawaiian Archaeology at Hawai'i Volcanoes National Park.

Dodge, E. S.
1939 Four Hawaiian Implements in the Peabody Museum of Salem. *Journal of the Polynesian Society* 48:156–157.

Doelle, William H., David A. Gregory, and Henry D. Wallace
1995 Classic Period Platform Mound Systems in Southern Arizona. In *The Roosevelt Community Development Study: New Perspectives on Tonto Basin Prehistory*, edited by Mark D. Elson, Miriam T. Stark, and David A. Gregory, Chapter 13:385–440. Anthropological Papers 15. Center for Desert Archaeology, Tucson, Arizona.

Donham, Theresa K.
2000 *Data Recovery Excavations at the Honokahua Burial Site, Land of Honokahua, Lahaina District, Island of Maui*. Paul H. Rosendahl, Ph.D., Hilo, Hawaii. Submitted to Kapalua Land Company, Ltd.

Doyle, Emma L.
1953 *Makua Laiana; the Story of Lorenzo Lyons, Lovingly Known to Hawaiians as Ka Makua Laiana, Haku Mele O Ka Aina Mauna (Father Lyons, Lyric Poet of the Mountain Country)*. Revised and enlarged. Honolulu.

Drennan, Robert D. and Christian E. Peterson
2012 Challenges for Comparative Study of Early Complex Societies. In *The Comparative Archaeology of Complex Societies*, edited by Michael E. Smith, pp. 62–87. Cambridge University Press, Cambridge.

Duff, Roger
1959 Neolithic Adzes of Eastern Polynesia. In *Anthropology of the South Seas*, edited by Derek Freeman and W. R. Geddes. T. Avery, 121–147. New Plymouth, New Zealand.

Dunnell, Robert C.
1970 Seriation Method and its Evaluation. *American Antiquity* 35:305–319.

Dye, David H.
2006 The Transformation of Mississippian Warfare: Four Case Studies from the Mid-South. In *The Archaeology of Warfare: Prehistories of Raiding and Conquest*, edited by Elizabeth N. Arkush and Mark D. Allen, pp. 101–147. University of Florida Press, Gainesville.

Dye, Thomas S.
1989 Tales of Two Cultures: Traditional Historical and Archaeological Interpretations of Hawaiian Prehistory. *Bishop Museum Occasional Papers* 29:3–22.

1992 The South Point Radiocarbon Dates 30 Years Later. *New Zealand Journal of Archaeology* 14:89–97.

2002 *Archaeological Data Recovery in the Barren Zone, Manini'ōwali and Kūki'o 2nd Ahupua'a, Kona, Hawai'i*. T. S. Dye & Colleagues, Archaeologists, Honolulu. Submitted to W/B Manini'ōwali.

2010 Traditional Hawaiian Surface Architecture: Absolute and Relative Dating. In *Research Designs for Hawaiian Archaeology: Agriculture, Architecture, Methodology*, edited by Thomas S. Dye. Special Publications 3, Chapter 2:93–155. Society for Hawaiian Archaeology, Honolulu.

2011a A Model-Based Age Estimate for Polynesian Colonization of Hawai'i. *Archaeology in Oceania* 46:130–138.

2011b The Tempo of Change in the Leeward Kohala Field System, Hawai'i Island. *Rapa Nui Journal* 25(2):21–30.

Dye, Thomas S. and Eric K. Komori

1992 A Pre-censal Population History of Hawai'i. *New Zealand Journal of Archaeology* 14:113–128.

Dye, Thomas S. and Jeffrey J. Pantaleo

2010 Age of the O18 Site, Hawai'i. *Archaeology in Oceania* 45:113–119.

Dye, Thomas S. and David W. Steadman

1990 Polynesian Ancestors and their Animal World. *American Scientist* 78:207–215.

Dye, Thomas S., Maurice Major, Michael E. Desilets, and MaryAnne B. Maigret

2002 *Archaeological Inventory Survey of Portions of Kekaha Kai State Park.* T. S. Dye & Colleagues, Archaeologists, Honolulu. Submitted to Group 70 International.

Earle, Timothy K.

1977 A Reappraisal of Redistribution: Complex Hawaiian Chiefdoms. In *Exchange Systems in Prehistory*. Studies in Archeology. Academic Press, New York.

1978 *Economic and Social Organization of a Complex Chiefdom: The Halelea District, Kaua'i, Hawaii.* Anthropological Papers 63. Museum of Anthropology, University of Michigan, Ann Arbor, Michigan.

1980 Prehistoric Irrigation in the Hawaiian Islands: An Evaluation of Evolutionary Significance. *Archaeology and Physical Anthropology in Oceania* 15:1–28.

1987 Specialization and the Production of Wealth: Hawaiian Chiefdoms and the Inka Empire. In *Specialization, Exchange, and Complex Societies*, edited by Elizabeth M. Brumfiel and Timothy K. Earle, pp. 64–75. Cambridge University Press, Cambridge and New York.

1997 *How Chiefs Come to Power: The Political Economy in Prehistory.* Stanford University Press, Stanford, California.

Earle, Timothy K. and Jonathon E. Ericson

1977 *Exchange Systems in Prehistory*. Studies in Archeology. Academic Press, New York.

Ellis, William

1979 *Journal of William Ellis: Narrative of a Tour of Hawaii, or Owhyhee: With Remarks on the History, Traditions, Manners, Customs, and Language of the Inhabitants of the Sandwich Islands.* Tuttle, Rutland, Vermont.

Emory, Kenneth P.

1924 *The Island of Lanai: A Survey of Native Culture.* Bernice P. Bishop Museum Bulletin 12. Bishop Museum Press, Honolulu.

1928 *Archaeology of Nihoa and Necker Islands.* Bernice P. Bishop Museum Bulletin 53. Bishop Museum Press, Honolulu.

1968 East Polynesian Relationships as Revealed through Adzes. In *Prehistoric Culture in Oceania: A Symposium*, edited by Ichiro Yawata and Yosihiko H. Sinoto, pp. 151–169. Bishop Museum Press, Honolulu.

Emory, Kenneth P., William J. Bonk, and Yosihiko H. Sinoto
  1968 *Hawaiian Archaeology: Fishhooks.* B. P. Bishop Museum Special Publication 47. Bishop Museum Press, Honolulu.
  1969 *Waiahukini Shelter, Site H8, Kaʻu, Hawaii.* Pacific Anthropological Records 7. Anthropology Department, B. P. Bishop Museum, Honolulu.
Emory, Kenneth P. and Yosihiko H. Sinoto
  1969 *Age of the Sites in the South Point Area, Kaʻu, Hawaii.* Pacific Anthropological Records 8. Anthropology Department, B. P. Bishop Museum, Honolulu.
Farber, Joseph M.
  1997 *Ancient Hawaiian Fishponds: Can Restoration Succeed on Molokai?* Neptune House Publications in association with the East-West Center's Pacific Islands Development Program, Encinitas, California.
Feinman, Gary M. and Joyce Marcus (editors)
  1998 *Archaic States.* School of American Research, Santa Fe, New Mexico.
Ferguson, R. Brian
  2006 Archaeology, Cultural Anthropology, and the Origins and Intensifications of War. In *The Archaeology of Warfare: Prehistories of Raiding and Conquest,* edited by Elizabeth N. Arkush and Mark D. Allen, pp. 469–525. University of Florida Press, Gainseville.
Field, Julie S. and Michael W. Graves
  2008 A New Chronology for Pololu Valley, Hawaiʻi Island: Occupational History and Agricultural Development. *Radiocarbon* 50(2):205–222.
Field, Julie S., Patrick V. Kirch, Kathy Kawelu, and Thegn N. Ladefoged
  2010 Households and Hierarchy: Domestic Modes of Production in Leeward Kohala, Hawaiʻi Island. *Journal of Island and Coastal Archaeology* 5(1):52–85.
Field, Julie S., Thegn N. Ladefoged, Warren D. Sharp, and Patrick V. Kirch
  2011 Residential Chronology, Household Subsistence, and the Emergence of Socioeconomic Territories in Leeward Kohala, Hawaiʻi Island. *Radiocarbon* 53(4):605–627.
Finney, Ben R.
  1979 *Hokuleʻa: The Way to Tahiti.* Dodd, Mead, New York.
Fitzpatrick, Scott M. and Richard Callaghan
  2009 Examining Dispersal Mechanisms for the Translocation of Chicken (*Gallus gallus*) from Polynesia to South America. *Journal of Archaeological Science* 36(2):214–223.
Fitzpatrick, Scott M., A. C. Caruso, and J. E. Peterson
  2006 Metal Tools and the Transformation of an Oceanic Exchange System. *Historical Archaeology* 40:9–27.
Flannery, Kent V.
  1998 The Ground Plans of Archaic States. In *Archaic States,* edited by Gary M. Feinman and Joyce Marcus, p. 15–57. School of American Research, Santa Fe, New Mexico.

Flexner, James L.
2010 Archaeology of the Recent Past at Kalawao: Landscape, Place, and Power in a Hawaiian Hansen's Disease Settlement. Ph.D. dissertation. University of California, Berkeley, Berkeley.
2012 An Institution That Was a Village: Archaeology and Social Life in the Hansen's Disease Settlement at Kalawao, Moloka'i, Hawai'i. *International Journal of Historical Archaeology* 16(1):135–163.
Fornander, Abraham
1916–1919 *Fornander Collection of Hawaiian Antiquities and Folklore*. Memoirs of the B. P. Bishop Museum 4–6. Translations revised and illustrated with notes by Thomas G. Thrum. Bishop Museum Press, Honolulu.
1969 *An Account of the Polynesian Race, its Origins and Migrations, and the Ancient History of the Hawaiian People to the Times of Kamehameha*. 3 vols. Originally published 1878–1885. Charles E. Tuttle, Rutland, Vermont.
1996 *Ancient History of the Hawaiian People to the Times of Kamehameha I*. Mutual, Honolulu.
Fowler, Melvin L.
1975 A Precolumbian Urban Center on the Mississippi. *Scientific American* 233:92–101.
Freycinet, Louis Claude Desaulses de, Ella L. Wiswell, and Marion Kelly
1978 *Hawaii in 1819: A Narrative Account*. Pacific Anthropological Records 26. Anthropology Department, B. P. Bishop Museum, Honolulu.
Friedman, Jonathan
1995 Global System, Globalization and the Parameters of Modernity. In *Global Modernities*, edited by Mike Featherstone, Scott Lash, and Roland Robertson. Sage Publications, London.
Gagné, Wayne C. and Linda W. Cuddihy
1990 Vegetation. In *Manual of the Flowering Plants of Hawai'i, pp.* 45–114. B. P. Bishop Museum Special Publication 83. University of Hawaii Press and Bishop Museum Press, Honolulu.
Garland, Anne W. H.
1996 Material Culture Change after EuroAmerican Contact in Honolulu, Hawai'i, Circa 1800–1850: A Selectionist Model for Diet and Tablewares. Ph.D. dissertation. University of Hawaii.
Gilman, P. A.
1987 Architecture as Artifact: Pit Structures and Pueblos in the American Southwest. *American Antiquity* 52:538–564.
Gongora, Jaime, Nicolas J. Rawlence, Victor A. Mobegi, Han Jianlin, Jose A. Alcalde, Jose T. Matus, Olivier Hanotte, Chris Moran, Jeremy J. Austin, Sean Ulm, Atholl J. Anderson, Greger Larson, and Alan Cooper
2008 Indo-European and Asian Origins for Chilean and Pacific Chickens Revealed by mtDNA. *Proceedings of the National Academy of Sciences* 105(30): 10308–10313.

Goodfellow, Susan T. and James A. Head

1995 *Archaeological Inventory Survey, Kaupulehu Mauka Lands, Golf Course II Area and Remaining Area, Land of Kaupulehu, North Kona District, Island of Hawaii (TMK:7–2–3:03)*. Paul H. Rosendahl, Ph.D., Hilo, Hawaii. Submitted to Potomac Investment Associates.

Goodfellow, Susan T., Peter M. Jensen, and Patrick Bower

1992 *Archaeological Mitigation Program. Phase II—Archaeological Data Recovery, Regent Kona Coast Resort, Land of Kukio 1st, North Kona District, Island of Hawaii (TMK:3–7–2–04:5, 16)*. Paul H. Rosendahl, Ph.D., Hilo, Hawaii. Submitted to PBR Hawaii.

Gordon, Elizabeth A.

1993 Screen Size and Differential Faunal Recovery: A Hawaiian Example. *Journal of Field Archaeology* 20:453–460.

Goto, Akira

1986 Prehistoric Ecology and Economy of Fishing in Hawaii: An Ethnoarchaeological Approach. PhD thesis. University of Hawaii.

Graves, Michael W. and David J. Addison

1995 The Polynesian Settlement of the Hawaiian Archipelago: Interpreting Models and Methods in Archaeological Interpretation. *World Archaeology* 26(3):380–399.

Graves, Michael W. and C. Kēhaunani Cachola-Abad

1996 Seriation as a Method of Chronologically Ordering Architectural Design Traits: An Example from Hawai'i. *Archaeology in Oceania* 31:19–32.

Graves, Michael W., Julie S. Field, and Windy K. McElroy

2005 An Overview of Site 50–30–01–196, Nu'alolo Kai, Kaua'i: Features, Excavations, Stratigraphy, and Chronology of Historic and Prehistoric Occupations. In *Na Mea Kahiko o Kaua'i: Archaeological Studies in Kaua'i*, edited by Mike T. Carson and Michael W. Graves, pp. 149–187. Special Publication 2. Society for Hawaiian Archaeology, Honolulu.

Graves, Michael W. and Windy K. McElroy

2005 Hawaiian Fishhook Classification, Identification, and Analysis, Nu'alolo Kai (Site 50–30–01–196), Kaua'i. In *Na Mea Kahiko o Kaua'i: Archaeological Studies in Kaua'i*, edited by Mike T. Carson and Michael W. Graves. Special Publication 2, pp. 188–211. Society for Hawaiian Archaeology, Honolulu.

Green, Roger C.

1971 The Chronology and Age of Sites at South Point, Hawaii. *Archaeology and Physical Anthropology in Oceania* 6(2):170–176.

1980 *Makaha Before 1880 AD Makaha Valley Historical Project, Report No. 5*. Pacific Anthropological Records 31. Anthropology Department, B. P. Bishop Museum, Honolulu.

1984 Settlement Pattern Studies in Oceania: An Introduction to a Symposium. *New Zealand Journal of Archaeology* 6:59–69.

2000 A Range of Disciplines Support a Dual Origin for the Bottle Gourd in the Pacific. *Journal of the Polynesian Society* 109(2):191–198.

2005   Sweet Potato Transfers in Polynesian Prehistory. In *The Sweet Potato in Oceania: A Reappraisal,* edited by Chris Ballard, Paula Brown, R. Michael Bourke, and Tracy Harwood, Chapter 5:43–62. Oceania Monograph 56. University of Sydney, Sydney, Australia.

Green, Roger C. (editor)

1969   *Makaha Valley Historical Project.* Pacific Anthropological Records 4. Anthropology Department, B. P. Bishop Museum, Honolulu.

1970   *Makaha Valley Historical Project: Interim Report No. 2.* Pacific Anthropological Records 10. Anthropology Department, B. P. Bishop Museum, Honolulu.

Handy, E. S. Craighill

1940   *The Hawaiian Planter.* Vol. 1. B.P. Bishop Museum Bulletin Number 161. Bishop Museum Press, Honolulu.

Handy, E. S. Craighill and Elizabeth Green Handy

1972   *Native Planters in Old Hawaii: Their Life, Lore, and Environment.* B. P. Bishop Museum Bulletin 233. With the collaboration of Mary Kawena Pukui. Bishop Museum Press, Honolulu.

Handy, E. S. Craighill and Mary Kawena Pukui

1972   *The Polynesian Family System in Ka-ʻu, Hawaiʻi.* Charles E. Tuttle, Tokyo.

Hartzell, Leslie L.

1997   Faunal Assemblages. In *Imu, Adzes, and Upland Agriculture: Inventory Survey Archaeology in North Hālawa Valley, Oʻahu,* Chapter 7:135–161. Anthropology Department, B. P. Bishop Museum, Honolulu. Submitted to State of Hawaii, Department of Transportation, Highways Division and U.S. Department of Transportation, Federal Highway Administration.

Hawaiʻi Biocomplexity Project Team

2010   The Hawaiʻi Biocomplexity Project in Retrospect. In *Roots of Conflict: Soils, Agriculture, and Sociopolitical Complexity in Ancient Hawaiʻi,* edited by Patrick V. Kirch, Chapter 8:163–171. Advanced Seminar Series. School for Advanced Research Press, Santa Fe, New Mexico.

Hillier, Bill and Julienne Hanson

1984   *The Social Logic of Space.* Cambridge University Press, Cambridge.

Hinds, Richard B.

1968   The Sandwich Islands, from Richard Brinsley Hinds' Journal of the Voyage of the *Sulphur* (1836–1842). *Hawaiian Journal of History* 2. Transcribed and edited by E. Alison Kay:102–135.

Holmes, Tommy

1981   *The Hawaiian Canoe.* Editions Limited, Honolulu.

Hommon, Robert J.

1970   Subzone 1C of Archaeological Zone 1 in the Lower Makaha Valley. In *Makaha Valley Historical Project: Interim Report No. 2,* edited by Roger C. Green. Pacific Anthropological Records 10. Anthropology Department, B. P. Bishop Museum, Honolulu.

1976   The Formation of Primitive States in Pre-contact Hawaii. Ph.D. dissertation. University of Arizona, Tucson.

1986   Social Evolution in Ancient Hawaii. In *Island Societies: Archaeological Approaches to Evolution and Transformation*, edited by Patrick V. Kirch, pp. 55–68. Cambridge University Press, Cambridge.

2010   Watershed: Testing the Limited Land Hypothesis. In *Research Designs for Hawaiian Archaeology*, edited by Thomas S. Dye, Chapter 1:1–92. Special Publications 3. Society for Hawaiian Archaeology, Honolulu.

Hooper, Antony and Judith Huntsman (editors)

1985   *Transformations of Polynesian Culture*. Memoirs of the Polynesian Society 45. Polynesian Society, Auckland, New Zealand.

Horrocks, Mark and Robert B. Rechtman

2009   Sweet Potato (*Ipomoea batatas*) and Banana (*Musa* sp.) Microfossils in Deposits from the Kona Field System, Island of Hawaii. *Journal of Archaeological Science* 36(5):1115–1126.

Hunt, Terry L.

2005   Archaeological Stratigraphy and Chronology at Nuʻalolo Kai, Nā Pali District, Kauaʻi. In *Na Mea Kahiko o Kauaʻi: Archaeological Studies in Kauaʻi*, edited by Mike T. Carson and Michael W. Graves, pp. 236–258. Special Publication 2. Society for Hawaiian Archaeology, Honolulu.

Hunt, Terry L. and Robert M. Holsen

1991   An Early Radiocarbon Chronology for the Hawaiian Islands: A Preliminary Analysis. *Asian Perspectives* 30:147–161.

ʻĪʻī, John Papa

1963   *Fragments of Hawaiian History*. Translated by Mary Kawena Pukui. Edited by Dorothy B. Barrère. Bishop Museum Press, Honolulu.

Inomata, Takeshi

2001   The Power and Ideology of Artistic Creation: Elite Craft Specialists in Classic Maya Society. *Current Anthropology* 42:321–349.

Irwin, Geoffrey

1992   *The Prehistoric Exploration and Colonisation of the Pacific*. Cambridge University Press, Cambridge.

Jackson, Frances Orel and United States

1966   Report on Kiʻilae Village, South Kona, Hawaii. Typescript in Hamilton Library, University of Hawaiʻi. Honolulu.

Jensen, Peter M.

1990   *Archaeological Data Recovery Program: Lots 1, 2, 6, 7, 17, 24, Waikoloa Beach Resort, Land of Anaehoomalu, South Kohala District, Island of Hawaii*. Prepared for Waikoloa Development Co. Paul H. Rosendahl, Ph.D., Hilo, Hawaii.

Jones, Sharyn and Patrick V. Kirch

2007   Indigenous Hawaiian Fishing Practices in Kahikinui, Maui: A Zooarchaeological Approach. *Hawaiian Archaeology* 11:39–53.

Judd, Walter
  1975 *Palaces and Forts of the Hawaiian Kingdom: From Thatch to American Floren-*
        tine. Pacific Books, Palo Alto, California.
Juvik, Sonia P. and James O. Juvik (editors)
  1998 *Atlas of Hawai'i.* Third. University of Hawaii Press, Honolulu.
Kaeppler, Adrienne L.
  1978 *"Artificial Curiosities": An Exposition of Native Manufactures Collected on the*
        Three Voyages of Captain James Cook, R.N. Bernice P. Bishop Museum Special Pub-
        lication 65. Bishop Museum Press, Honolulu.
  1985 Hawaiian Art and Society: Traditions and Transformations. In *Transformations*
        of Polynesian Culture, edited by Antony Hooper and Judith Huntsman, pp.
        105–131. Memoirs of the Polynesian Society 45. Polynesian Society, Auckland,
        New Zealand.
Kahā'ulelio, Daniel
  2006 *Ka 'Oihana Lawai'a: Hawaiian Fishing Traditions.* Translated by Mary Kawena
        Pukui and edited by M. Puakea Nogelmeier. Bishop Museum, Honolulu.
Kahn, Jenny G., Peter R. Mills, Steven Lundblad, John Holson, and Patrick V. Kirch
  2009 Tool Production at the Nu'u Quarry, Maui, Hawaiian Islands: Manufacturing
        Sequences and Energy Dispersive X-ray Analyses. *New Zealand Journal of Archae-*
        ology 30:135–165.
Kamakau, Samuel M.
  1961 *Ruling Chiefs of Hawaii.* Kamehameha Schools Press, Honolulu.
  1964 *Ka Po'e Kahiko: The People of Old.* B. P. Bishop Museum Special Publication
        51. Bishop Museum Press, Honolulu.
  1976 *The Works of the People of Old: Na Hana a ka Po'e Kahiko.* B. P. Bishop
        Museum Special Publication 61. Translated from the Newspaper *Ke Au 'Oko'a* by
        Mary Kawena Pukui. Arranged and edited by Dorothy B. Barrère. Bishop
        Museum Press, Honolulu.
Kamehiro, Stacy L.
  2007 Hawaiian Quilts: Chiefly Self-Representations in Nineteenth-Century
        Hawai'i. *Pacific Arts: The Journal of the Pacific Arts Association,* Vols. 3–5.
Kawelu, Kathleen L.
  2007 A Sociopolitical History of Hawaiian Archaeology: Kuleana and Commit-
        ment. Ph.D. dissertation. University of California, Berkeley, Berkeley, California.
Keeley, Lawrence
  1996 *War before Civilization.* Oxford University Press, New York.
Kikiloi, Kekuewa
  2010 Rebirth of an Archipelago: Sustaining a Hawaiian Cultural Identity for People
        and Homeland. *Hūlili* 6:73–115.
Kikuchi, William K.
  1976 Hawaiian Aquacultural System. Ph.D. dissertation. University of Arizona,
        Tucson.

Kirch, Patrick V.

1971   Archaeological Excavations at Palauea, Southeast Maui, Hawaiian Islands. *Archaeology and Physical Anthropology in Oceania* 6:62–86.

1972   Five Triangular Adzes from Haiku, Maui, Hawaiian Islands. *New Zealand Archaeological Association Newsletter* 15(4):140–143.

1977   Valley Agricultural Systems in Prehistoric Hawaii: An Archaeological Consideration. *Asian Perspectives* 20(2):246–280.

1982a The Ecology of Marine Exploitation in Prehistoric Hawaii. *Human Ecology* 10:455–476.

1982b The Impact of the Prehistoric Polynesians on the Hawaiian Ecosystem. *Pacific Science* 36:1–14.

1984   *The Evolution of the Polynesian Chiefdoms*. New Studies in Archaeology. Cambridge University Press, Cambridge.

1985   *Feathered Gods and Fishhooks: An Introduction to Hawaiian Archaeology and Prehistory*. University of Hawaii Press, Honolulu.

1990   The Evolution of Sociopolitical Complexity in Prehistoric Hawaii: An Assessment of the Archaeological Evidence. *Journal of World Prehistory* 4:311–345.

1994   *The Wet and the Dry: Irrigation and Agricultural Intensification in Polynesia*. University of Chicago Press, Chicago.

2000   *On the Road of the Winds: An Archaeological History of the Pacific Islands Before European Contact*. University of California Press, Berkeley.

2004   Temple Sites in Kahikinui, Maui, Hawaiian Islands: Their Orientations Decoded. *Antiquity* 78:102–114.

2010a *How Chiefs Became Kings: Divine Kingship and the Rise of Archaic States in Ancient Hawai'i*. University of California Press, Berkeley.

2010b The Archaeology of Dryland Farming Systems in Southeastern Maui. In *Roots of Conflict: Soils, Agriculture, and Sociopolitical Complexity in Ancient Hawai'i*, edited by Patrick V. Kirch, Chapter 4:65–88. Advanced Seminar Series. School for Advanced Research Press, Santa Fe, New Mexico.

2011   When Did the Polynesians Settle Hawai'i? A Review of 150 Years of Scholarly Inquiry and a Tentative Answer. *Hawaiian Archaeology* 12:3–26.

Kirch, Patrick V. (editor)

2010   *Roots of Conflict: Soils, Agriculture, and Sociopolitical Complexity in Ancient Hawai'i*. Advanced Seminar Series. School for Advanced Research Press, Santa Fe, New Mexico.

Kirch, Patrick V. and Sara L. Collins

1989   Faunal Assemblages of the Anahulu Rockshelter Sites. In *Prehistoric Hawaiian Occupation in the Anahulu Valley, O'ahu Island: Excavations in Three Inland Rockshelters*, edited by Patrick V. Kirch, Chapter 4:61–72. Contributions of the University of California Archaeological Research Facility 47. Department of Anthropology, University of California at Berkeley, Berkeley.

Kirch, Patrick V. and Roger C. Green
 2001 *Hawaiki, Ancestral Polynesia: An Essay in Historical Anthropology.* Cambridge
    University Press, Cambridge.
Kirch, Patrick V. and Marion Kelly (editors)
 1975 *Prehistory and Ecology in a Windward Hawaiian Valley: Halawa Valley,
    Molokai.* Pacific Anthropological Records 24. Anthropology Department, B. P.
    Bishop Museum, Honolulu.
Kirch, Patrick V. and Mark D. McCoy
 2007 Reconfiguring the Hawaiian Cultural Sequence: Results of Re-dating the
    Hālawa Dune Site (Mo-A1-3), Moloka'i Island. *Journal of the Polynesian Society*
    116:385–406.
Kirch, Patrick V. and Sharyn J. O'Day
 2003 New Archaeological Insights into Food and Status: A Case Study from Pre-
    Contact Hawai'i. *World Archaeology* 34(3):484–497.
Kirch, Patrick V. and Marshall D. Sahlins
 1992 *Anahulu: The Anthropology of History in the Kingdom of Hawaii.* 2 vols. Uni-
    versity of Chicago Press, Chicago.
Kirch, Patrick V. and Warren D. Sharp
 2005 Coral ^{230}Th Dating of the Imposition of a Ritual Contral Hierarchy in Pre-
    contact Hawaii. *Science* 307:102–103.
Kirch, Patrick V., Sharon O'Day, James Coil, Maury Morgenstein, Kathy Kawelu, and
    M. Millerstrom
 2003 The Kaupikiawa Rockshelter, Kalaupapa Peninsula, Moloka'i: New Investiga-
    tions and Reinterpretation of its Significance for Hawaiian Prehistory. *People and
    Culture in Oceania* 19:1–27.
Kirch, Patrick V., Sidsel Millerstrom, Sharyn Jones, and Mark D. McCoy
 2010 Dwelling Among the Gods: A Late Pre-Contact Priest's House in Kahikinui,
    Maui, Hawaiian Islands. *Journal of Pacific Archaeology* 1(2):145–160.
Kirch, Patrick V., Peter R. Mills, Steven P. Lundblad, John Sinton, and Jennifer G. Kahn
 2012 Interpolity Exchange of Basalt Tools Facilitated via Elite Control in Hawaiian
    Archaic States. *Proceedings of the National Academy of Sciences* 109(4):1056–1061.
Klieger, Paul C.
 1998 *Moku'ula: Maui's Sacred Island.* Bishop Museum Press, Honolulu.
Kolb, Michael J.
 1991 Social Power, Chiefly Authority, and Ceremonial Architecture in an Island
    Polity, Maui, Hawaii. PhD thesis. University of California, Los Angeles.
 1994 Monumentality and the Rise of Religious Authority in Precontact Hawai'i.
    Current Anthropology 34:521–547.
 2006 The Origins of Monumental Architecture in Ancient Hawai'i. *Current
    Anthropology* 47(4):657–665.
 2012 The Genesis of Monuments in Island Societies. In *The Comparative Archaeol-
    ogy of Complex Societies,* edited by Michael E. Smith, pp. 138–164. Cambridge
    University Press, Cambridge.

Kolb, Michael J. and Boyd Dixon
2002 Landscapes of War: Rules and Conventions of Conflict in Ancient Hawaii (and elsewhere). *American Antiquity* 67:514–534.

Kosaki, R. H.
1954 *Konohiki Fishing Rights.* Report. Legislative Reference Bureau, University of Hawaii, Honolulu.

Kraus-Friedberg, Chana
2011 Across the Pacific: Transnational Context in the Japanese Plantation Workers' Cemetery in Pahala, Hawaiʻi. *International Journal of Historical Archaeology* 15(3):381–408.

Krauss, Beatrice H.
1993 *Plants in Hawaiian Culture.* University of Hawaii Press, Honolulu.

Kuykendall, Ralph S.
1938 *The Hawaiian Kingdom.* University of Hawaii, Honolulu.

Ladd, Edmund J.
1973 Kaneaki Temple Site—an Excavation Report. In *Makaha Valley Historical Project: Interim Report No. 4,* edited by Edmund J. Ladd. Pacific Anthropological Records 19, Chapter 1:1–30. Anthropology Department, B. P. Bishop Museum, Honolulu.

1985 *Hale-o-Keawe Archaeological Report.* Western Archaeological and Conservation Center Publications in Anthropology 33. Edited by Gary F. Somers. National Park Service, U.S. Department of the Interior, Tucson, Arizona.

Ladefoged, Thegn N.
1991 Hawaiian Architectural Transformations During the Early Historic Era. *Asian Perspectives* 30(1):57–70.

Ladefoged, Thegn N. and Michael W. Graves
2000 Evolutionary Theory and the Historical Development of Dry-Land Agriculture in North Kohala, Hawaiʻi. *American Antiquity* 65(3):423–448.

2006 The Formation of Hawaiian Territories. In *Archaeology of Oceania: Australia and the Pacific Islands,* edited by Ian Lilley, Chapter 13:259–283. Blackwell Studies in Global Archaeology 8. Blackwell, Oxford, United Kingdom.

2008 Variable Development of Dryland Agriculture in Hawaiʻi: A Fine-Grained Chronology from the Kohala Field System, Hawaiʻi Island. *Current Anthropology* 49(5):771–802.

Ladefoged, Thegn N., Michael W. Graves, and James H. Coil
2005 The Introduction of Sweet Potato in Polynesia: Early Remains in Hawaiʻi. *Journal of the Polynesian Society* 114(4):359–373.

Ladefoged, Thegn N., Michael W. Graves, and Mark D. McCoy
2003 Archaeological Evidence for Agricultural Development in Kohala, Island of Hawaii. *Journal of Archaeological Science* 30:923–940.

Ladefoged, Thegn N., Patrick V. Kirch, Samuel M. Gon III, Oliver A. Chadwick, Anthony S. Hartshorn, and Peter M. Vitousek

2009 Opportunities and Constraints for Intensive Agriculture in the Hawaiian Archipelago Prior to European Contact. *Journal of Archaeological Science* 36:2374–2383.

Ladefoged, Thegn N., Patrick V. Kirch, Oliver A. Chadwick, Sam M. Gon III, Anthony S. Hartshorn, and Sara C. Hotchkiss

2010 Hawaiian Agro-ecosystems and their Spatial Distribution. In *Roots of Conflict: Soils, Agriculture, and Sociopolitical Complexity in Ancient Hawai'i*, edited by Patrick V. Kirch, Chapter 3:45–63. Advanced Seminar Series. School for Advanced Research Press, Santa Fe, New Mexico.

Lam, Maivan C.

1989 The Kuleana Act Revisited: The Survival of Traditional Hawaiian Commoner Rights in Land. *Washington Law Review* 64:233–288.

Lass, Barbara

1994 *Hawaiian Adze Production and Distribution: Implications for the Development of Chiefdoms*. Institute of Archaeology Monograph 37. University of California, Los Angeles.

1998 Crafts, Chiefs, and Commoners: Production and Control in Precontact Hawaii. In *Craft and Social Identity*, edited by Cathy L. Costin and Rita P. Wright, pp. 19–30. Archaeological Papers of the American Anthropological Association 8. American Anthropological Association, Arlington, Virginia.

Lawrence, S. and N. Shepherd

2006 Historical Archaeology and Colonialism. In *The Cambridge Companion to Historical Archaeology*. Cambridge University Press, Cambridge.

Leach, Helen M.

1993 The Role of Major Quarries in Polynesian Prehistory. In *The Evolution and Organization of Prehistoric Society in Polynesia*, edited by Michael W. Graves and Roger C. Green, pp. 33–42. Monographs of the New Zealand Archaeological Association 19. New Zealand Archaeological Association, Auckland.

LeBlanc, Steven A.

1999 *Prehistoric Warfare in the American Southwest*. University of Utah Press, Salt Lake City.

Lebo, Susan A. and James M. Bayman

2001 New Perspectives on Kaniakapupu, Nu'uanu Valley, O'ahu: Undertaking Archaeological Fieldwork within the Framework of a Hui. In *Pacific 2000: Proceedings of the Fifth International Conference on Easter Island and the Pacific*, edited by Christopher M. Stevenson, Georgia Lee, and Frank J. Morin, pp. 157–161. Easter Island Foundation and Bearsville Press, Los Osos, California.

Lebo, Susan A. and Kevin T. M. Johnson
2007   Geochemical Sourcing of Rock Specimens and Stone Artifacts from Nihoa and Necker Islands, Hawai'i. *Journal of Archaeological Science* 34:858–871.

Lebot, Vincent, Mark Merlin, and Lamont Lindstrom
1992   *Kava: The Pacific Drug.* Yale University Press, New Haven, Connecticut.

Lebot, Vincent, Ed Johnston, Qun Yi Zheng, Doug McKern, and Dennis J. McKenna
1999   Morphological, Phytochemical, and Genetic Variation in Hawaiian Cultivars of 'Awa (Kava, *Piper methysticum*, Piperaceae). *Economic Botany* 53(4):407–418.

Ledyard, John
1964   *Journal of Captain Cook's Last Voyage.* Oregon State University Press, Corvallis.

Levison, Michael, R. Gerard Ward, and John W. Webb
1973   *The Settlement of Polynesia: A Computer Simulation.* With the assistance of Trevor I. Fenner and W. Alan Sentance. The University of Minnesota Press, Minneapolis.

Libby, Willard F.
1951   Radiocarbon Dates, II. *Science* 114:295.

Liller, William
2000   Necker Island, Hawai'i: Astronomical Implications of an Island Located at the Tropic of Cancer. *Rapa Nui Journal* 14:103–105.

Linnekin, Jocelyn
1987   Statistical Analysis of the Great *Māhele*: Some Preliminary Findings. *Journal of Pacific History* 22:15–33.

1988   Who Made the Feather Cloaks? A Problem in Hawaiian Gender Relations. *Journal of the Polynesian Society* 97(3):265–280.

1990   *Sacred Queens and Women of Consequence: Rank, Gender, and Colonialism in the Hawaiian Islands.* University of Michigan Press, Ann Arbor.

Lorence, David H. and Kenneth R. Wood
1994   *Kanaloa*, a New Genus of Fabaceae (Mimosidae) from Hawaii. *Novon* 4(2):137–145.

Lundblad, Steven P., Peter R. Mills, and K. Hon
2008   Analyzing Archaeological Basalt Using Non-destructive Energy Dispersive X-ray Fluorescence (EDXRF): Effects of Post-depositional Chemical Weathering and Sample Size on Analytical Precision. *Archaeometry* 50:1–11.

MacKenzie, Melody K.
1991   Historical Background. In *Native Hawaiian Rights Handbook*, edited by Melody Kapilialoha MacKenzie, Chapter 1:3–25. Native Hawaiian Legal Corporation and Office of Hawaiian Affairs, Honolulu.

Malo, David
1951   *Hawaiian Antiquities (Moolelo Hawaii).* 2nd ed. B. P. Bishop Museum Special Publication 2. Translated by Nathaniel B. Emerson. Bishop Museum Press, Honolulu.

1996 *Ka Moʻolelo Hawaiʻi: Hawaiian Traditions.* Translated by Malcolm Naea Chun. First Peopleʻs Productions, Honolulu.

Maly, Kepā and Onaona Maly

2003 *Ka Hana Lawaiʻa a me nā Koʻa of na Kai ʻEwalu: A History of Fishing Practices and Marine Fisheries of the Hawaiian Islands.* Compiled from native Hawaiian traditions, historical accounts, government communications, *kamaʻaina* testimony, and ethnography. Kumu Pono Associates, Hilo, HI. Submitted to the Nature Conservancy.

Masse, W. Bruce

1995 The Celestial Basis of Civilization. *Vistas in Astronomy* 39:463–477.

Mathieu, J. R. and D. A. Meyer

1997 Comparing Axe Heads of Stone, Bronze, and Steel: Studies in Experimental Archaeology. *Journal of Field Archaeology* 24:333–351.

McAllister, J. Gilbert

1933a *Archaeology of Kahoolawe.* Bernice P. Bishop Museum Bulletin 115. Bishop Museum Press, Honolulu.

1933b *Archaeology of Oahu.* Bermice P. Bishop Museum Bulletin 104. Bishop Museum Press, Honolulu.

McClellan, E.

1950 Holokū and Muʻumuʻu. *Forecast Magazine.* Outrigger Canoe Club, Honolulu:12.

McCoy, Mark D.

2005 The Development of the Kalaupapa Field System, Molokaʻi Island, Hawaiʻi. *Journal of the Polynesian Society* 114(4):339–358.

2011 Geochemical Characterization of Volcanic Glass from Puʻu Waʻawaʻa, Hawaiʻi Island. *Rapa Nui Journal* 25(2):41–49.

McCoy, Mark D., Michael W. Graves, and Gail Murakami

2010 Introduction of Breadfruit (*Artocarpus altilis*) to the Hawaiian Islands. *Economic Botany* 64:374–381.

McCoy, Mark D., Thegn N. Ladefoged, Michael W. Graves, and Jesse W. Stephen

2011 Strategies for Constructing Religious Authority in Ancient Hawaiʻi. *Antiquity* 85:927–941.

McCoy, Patrick C.

1986 *Archaeological Investigations in the Hopukani and Liloe Springs Area of the Mauna Kea Adze Quarry.* Prepared for U.S. Army Engineer Division, Pacific Ocean. Anthropology Department, B. P. Bishop Museum, Honolulu.

1990 Subsistence in a ʻNon-subsistenceʻ Environment: Factors of Production in a Hawaiian Alpine Desert Quarry. In *Pacific Production Systems: Approaches to Economic Prehistory,* edited by D. E. Yen and J. M. J. Mummery, *pp.* 85–119. Occasional Papers in Prehistory 18. Department of Prehistory, Research School of Pacific Studies, The Australian National University, Canberra.

1999 Neither Here nor There: A Rites of Passage Site on the Eastern Fringes of the Mauna Kea Adze Quarry, Hawaiʻi. *Hawaiian Archaeology* 7:11–34.

2011 Signs of a Divine Reality: The Materiality of Bird Cook Stones (*Pōhaku 'Eho*) from the Dry Interior Uplands and Mountainous Regions of the Island of Hawai'i. *Hawaiian Archaeology* 12:65–107.

McCoy, Patrick C., Marshall I. Weisler, J-X. Zhao, and Y-X. Feng
2009 ^{230}Th Dates for Dedicatory Corals from a Remote Alpine Desert Adze Quarry on Mauna Kea, Hawai'i. *Antiquity* 83:445–457.

McElroy, Windy K.
2004 Poi Pounders of Kaua'i Island, Hawai'i: Variability through Time and Space. *Hawaiian Archaeology* 9:25–49.

2007 The Development of Irrigated Agriculture in Wailau Valley, Moloka'i Island. Ph.D. dissertation. University of Hawai'i.

McElroy, Windy K., Thomas S. Dye, and Elaine H. R. Jourdane
2006 *Archaeological Monitoring and Investigations During Installation of Leach Fields at Bellows Air Force Station and Hickam Air Force Base, Waimānalo, Ko'olaupoko, and Moanalua, Kona, O'ahu.* T. S. Dye & Colleagues, Archaeologists, Honolulu. Submitted to Shaw Environmental.

McGerty, Leann, Michael F. Dega, and Robert L. Spear
1997 *Archaeological Excavations at Kuwili Fishpond, Site of the Proposed Liliha Civic Center, Kalihi-Palama, O'ahu, Hawai'i.* Scientific Consultant Services, Honolulu. Submitted to Okita Kunimitsu and Associates.

Meech, K. J. and F. X. Warther
1996 First Beginnings: Astronomy and Cosmic Architecture in Ancient Hawaii. In *Astronomical Traditions in Past Cultures*, edited by Veselina Koleva and Dimitŭr N. Kolev, pp. 25–33. Proceedings of the First Annual General Meeting of the European Society for Astronomy in Culture (SEAC), Smolyan, Bulgaria, 31 August–2 September 1993. Institute of Astronomy, Bulgarian Academy of Sciences; National Astronomical Observatory, Rozhen, Sofia.

Mills, Peter R.
1996 Transformations of a Structure: The Archaeology and Ethnohistory of a Russian Fort in a Hawaiian Chiefdom, Waimea, Kaua'i. Ph.D. dissertation. University of California, Berkeley.

2002a *Hawaii's Russian Adventure: A New Look at Old History.* University of Hawaii Press, Honolulu.

2002b Social Integration and the Ala Loa: Reconsidering the Significance of Trails in Hawaiian Exchange. *Asian Perspectives* 41:148–166.

2009 Folk Housing in the Middle of the Pacific: Architectural Lime, Creolized Ideologies, and Expressions of Power in 19th-century Hawaii. In *Materiality of Individuality*, edited by Carolyn L. White. Springer, New York.

Mills, Peter R., Steven P. Lundblad, Jacob G. Smith, Patrick C. McCoy, and Sean P. Naleimaile
2008 Science and Sensitivity: A Geochemical Characterization of the Mauna Kea Adze Quarry Complex. *American Antiquity* 73:743–758.

Mills, Peter R., Steven P. Lundblad, Julie S. Field, Alan B. Carpenter, Windy K. McElroy, and P. Ross
  2010   Geochemical Sourcing of Basalt Artifacts from Kaua'i, Hawaiian Islands. *Journal of Archaeological Science* 37:3385–3393.
Mills, Peter R., Steven P. Lundblad, Ken Hon, Jadelyn J. Moniz-Nakamura, Elizabeth L. Kahahane, Adrian Drake-Raue, Tanya M. Souza, and Richard Wei
  2011   Reappraising Craft Specialization and Exchange in Pre-Contact Hawai'i through Non-destructive Sourcing of Basalt Adze Debitage. *Journal of Pacific Archaeology* 2(2):79–92.
Mintmier, Melanie A.
  2007   Adze Production in Maui: Analysis of Lithic Materials from the West Rim of Haleakala. *Hawaiian Archaeology* 11:3–17.
Mintmier, Melanie A., Peter R. Mills, and Steven P. Lundblad
  2012   Energy-dispersive X-ray Fluorescence Analysis of Haleakalā Basalt Adze Quarry Materials, Maui, Hawai'i. *Journal of Archaeological Science* 39(3):615–623.
Moniz-Nakamura, Jadelyn J., Kathleen Sherry, and Laila Tamimi
  1998   Foraging for Food? Prehistoric Pit Features at Pōhakuloa, Hawai'i Island. *Rapa Nui Journal* 12(4):110–117.
Moniz, Jadelyn J.
  1997   The Role of Seabirds in Hawaiian Subsistence: Implications for Interpreting Avian Extinction and Extirpation in Polynesia. *Asian Perspectives* 36(1):27–50.
Morgenstein, M. and Thomas J. Riley
  1974   Hydration-Rind Dating of Basaltic Glass: A New Method for Archaeological Chronologies. *Asian Perspectives* 17:145–159.
Mulrooney, Mara A. and Thegn N. Ladefoged
  2005   Hawaiian *Heiau* and Agricultural Production in the Kohala Dryland Field System. *Journal of the Polynesian Society* 114(1):45–67.
Murra, J. V.
  1962   Cloth and its Functions in the Inca State. *American Anthropologist* 64:710–728.
Newman, T. Stell
  1970   *Hawaiian Fishing and Farming on the Island of Hawaii in* AD *1778*. Department of Land and Natural Resources, Division of State Parks, Honolulu.
Nogelmeier, Puakea
  2010   *Mai Pa'a i ka Leo: Historical Voice in Hawaiian Primary Materials*. Bishop Museum Press, Honolulu.
O'Day, Sharyn J.
  2001   Excavations at the Kipapa Rockshelter, Kahikinui, Maui, Hawai'i. *Asian Perspectives* 40(2):279–304.
O'Leary, Owen L.
  2005   Analysis of the Nu'alolo Kai 1/4-inch Fishbone Assemblage, Na Pali Coast, Kaua'i. In *Na Mea Kahiko o Kaua'i: Archaeological Studies in Kaua'i*, edited by

Mike T. Carson and Michael W. Graves, pp. 259–274. Special Publication 2. Society for Hawaiian Archaeology, Honolulu.

Oliver, Douglas L.
2002 *Polynesia in Early Historic Times*. Bess Press, Honolulu.

Olson, Larry
1983 Hawaiian Volcanic Glass Applied 'Dating' and 'Sourcing': Archaeological Context. In *Archaeological Investigations of the Mudlane-Waimea-Kawaihae Road Corridor, Island of Hawai'i: An Interdisciplinary Study of an Environmental Transect*, edited by Jeffery T. Clark and Patrick V. Kirch, pp. 325–340. Departmental Report Series 83–1. Anthropology Department, B. P. Bishop Museum, Honolulu.

Olszewski, Deborah I.
2007 Interpreting Activities in North Hālawa Valley, O'ahu: Adze Recycling and Resharpening. *Hawaiian Archaeology* 11:18–32.

Osorio, Jonathan K. K.
2002 *Dismembering Lāhui: A History of the Hawaiian Nation to 1887*. University of Hawai'i Press, Honolulu.

Pauketat, Timothy R.
2005 The Forgotten History of the Mississippians. In *North American Archaeology*, edited by Timothy R. Pauketat and Diana DiPaolo Loren, p. 187–211. Blackwell Publishing, Malden, Massachusetts.
2007 *Chiefdoms and Other Archaeological Delusions*. AltaMira Press, Lanham, Maryland.

Pearsall, Deborah M. and Michael K. Trimble
1984 Identifying Past Agricultural Activity through Soil Phytolith Analysis: A Case Study from the Hawaiian Islands. *Journal of Archaeological Science* 11(2):119–133.

Pearson, Richard J., Patrick V. Kirch, and Michael Pietrusewsky
1971 An Early Prehistoric Site at Bellows Beach, Waimanalo, Oahu, Hawaiian Islands. *Archaeology and Physical Anthropology in Oceania* 6(3):204–234.

Pels, P.
1997 The Anthropology of Colonialism: Culture, History, and the Emergence of Western Governmentality. *Annual Review of Anthropology* 26:163–183.

Peterson, C. E.
1964 Pioneer Architects and Builders of Honolulu. *Seventy Second Annual Report of the Hawaiian Historical Society for the Year 1963*.

Pfaffenberger, B.
1992 Social Anthropology of Technology. *Annual Review of Anthropology* 21:491–516.

Pfeffer, Michael T.
2001 The Engineering and Evolution of Hawaiian Fishhooks. In *Posing Questions for a Scientific Archaeology*, edited by Terry L. Hunt, Carl P. Lipo, and Sarah L. Sterling, Chapter 3:73–95. Bergin & Garvey, Westport, Connecticut.

Portlock, Nathaniel
1968 [1789] *A Voyage Round the World ... Performed in 1785, 1786, 1787 and 1788*. Da Capo Press, New York.

Preza, Donovan C.

2010 The Empirical Writes Back: Re-examining Hawaiian Dispossession Resulting from the Māhele of 1848. MA thesis. University of Hawaiʻi, Honolulu.

Public Broadcasting Service

1999 Nainoa on Wayfinding. Electronic document, http://www.pbs.org/wayfinders/wayfinding3.html, accessed January 23, 2013.

Rapoport, Amos

1969 *House Form and Culture.* Prentice-Hall, Englewood Cliffs, New Jersey.

Reinman, Fred M. and Jeffrey J. Pantaleo

1998 *Archaeological Investigations of Two Work Areas for the Legacy Resource Management Program at Pohakuloa Training Area, Island of Hawaiʻi.* Garcia and Associates, Honolulu. Submitted to U.S. Army Engineer District, Honolulu.

Renfrew, Colin

1977 Alternative Models for Exchange and Spatial Distribution. In *Exchange Systems in Prehistory,* pp. 71–90. Studies in Archeology. Academic Press, New York.

Rensel, Jan

1997 *Home in the Islands: Housing and Social Change in the Pacific.* University of Hawaiʻi Press, Honolulu.

Rieth, Timothy M., Terry L. Hunt, Carl Lipo, and Janet M. Wilmshurst

2011 The 13th Century Polynesian Colonization of Hawaiʻi Island. *Journal of Archaeological Science* 38:2740–2749.

Riley, Thomas J.

1975 Survey and Excavations of the Aboriginal Agricultural System. In *Prehistory and Ecology in a Windward Hawaiian Valley: Halawa Valley, Molokai,* edited by Patrick V. Kirch and Marion Kelly, pp. 79–116. Pacific Anthropological Records 24. Anthropology Department, B. P. Bishop Museum, Honolulu.

Rolett, Barry V. and Eric Conte

1995 Renewed Investigation of the Haʻatuatua Dune (Nukuhiva, Marquesas Islands): A Key Site in Polynesian Prehistory. *Journal of the Polynesian Society* 104(2):195–228.

Rose, Roger G.

1980 *A Museum to Instruct and Delight: William T. Brigham and the Founding of Bernice Pauahi Bishop Museum.* Bernice P. Bishop Museum Special Publication 68. Bishop Museum Press, Honolulu.

1992 *Reconciling the Past: Two Basketry Kāʻai and the Legendary Līloa and Lonoikamakahiki.* Bishop Museum Bulletin in Anthropology 5. Bishop Museum Press, Honolulu.

Rose, Roger G., Sheila Conant, and E. P. Kjellgren

1993 Hawaiian Standing Kāhili in the Bishop Museum: An Ethnological and Biological Analysis. *Journal of the Polynesian Society* 102:273–304.

Rosendahl, Paul H.

1972 Aboriginal Agriculture and Residence Patterns in Upland Lapakahi, Island of Hawaii. Ph.D. dissertation. University of Hawaii, Honolulu.

1994 Aboriginal Hawaiian Structural Remains and Settlement Patterns in the Upland Agricultural Zone at Lapakahi, Island of Hawai'i. *Hawaiian Archaeology* 3:14–70.

Ruggles, Clive L. N.

1999 Astronomy, Oral Literature, and Landscape in Ancient Hawaii. *Archaeoastronomy: The Journal of Astronomy in Culture* 14:33–86.

2001 Heiau Orientations and Alignments on Kaua'i. *Archaeoastronomy: The Journal of Astronomy in Culture* 16:46–82.

Sahlins, Marshall D.

1972 *Stone Age Economics*. Aldine, Chicago.

1981 The Stranger King: Or Dumèzil Among the Fijians. *Journal of Pacific History* 16(3):107–132.

2008 The Stranger-King or, Elementary Forms of the Politics of Life. *Indonesia and the Malay World* 36(105):177–199.

Sai, D. Keanu

2011 *Ua Mau Ke Ea, Sovereignty Endures: An Overview of the Political and Legal History of the Hawaiian Islands*. Pū'ā Foundation, Honolulu.

Salisbury, Richard F.

1962 *From Stone to Steel: Economic Consequences of a Technological Change in New Guinea*. Melbourne University Press on behalf of the Australian National University, Victoria, Australia.

Sandler, Rob, Frank S. Haines, and Julie Mehta

1993 *Architecture in Hawai'i: A Chronological Survey*. Mutual and Coral House, Honolulu.

Schiffer, Michael B.

2004 Studying Technological Change: A Behavioral Perspective. *World Archaeology* 36:579–585.

Schilt, Rose

1984 *Subsistence and Conflict in Kona, Hawai'i: An Archaeological Study of the Kuakini Highway Realignment Corrridor*. Departmental Report Series 84–1. Anthropology Department, B. P. Bishop Museum, Honolulu.

Schmitt, Robert C.

1981 Some Construction and Housing Firsts in Hawai'i. *The Hawaiian Journal of History* 15:101–112.

Schuster, Laura C.

1992 *Bulldozers and Archaeology at John Young's Homestead: Archaeology at Pu'ukohola Heiau National Historic Site*. Pacific Area Office, National Park Service, U.S. Department of the Interior, Honolulu.

Service, Elman R.

1962 *Primitive Social Organization: An Evolutionary Perspective*. Random House, New York.

Sharp, Andrew

1963 *Ancient Voyagers in Polynesia*. Angus and Robertson, Sydney.

Sharp, L.

1952 Steel Axes for Stone Age Australians. In *Human Problems in Technological Change, pp.* 69–81. Russell Sage Foundation, New York.

Silva, Noenoe K.

2000 *He Kānāwai E Ho'opau I Na Hula Kuolo Hawai'i*: The Political Economy of Banning the Hula. *The Hawaiian Journal of History* 34:29–48.

Sinoto, Yosihiko H.

1968 Chronology of Hawaiian Fishhooks. In *Hawaiian Archaeology: Fishhooks, pp.* 58–62. B. P. Bishop Museum Special Publication 47. Bishop Museum Press, Honolulu.

1991 A Revised System for the Classification and Coding of Hawaiian Fishhooks. *Bishop Museum Occasional Papers* 31:85–105.

Sinton, John M. and Yosihiko H. Sinoto

1997 A Geochemical Database for Polynesian Adze Studies. In *Prehistoric Long-Distance Interaction in Oceania: An Interdisciplinary Approach*, edited by Marshall I. Weisler, Chapter 11:194–204. New Zealand Archaeological Association Monograph 21. New Zealand Archaeological Association, Auckland.

Six, Janet L.

2005 The Ahupua'a of Hīlea: A Contested Landscape in the District of Ka'ū. MA thesis. Columbia University, New York.

Smith, Michael E. (editor)

2012 *The Comparative Archaeology of Complex Societies*. Cambridge University Press, Cambridge.

Spielmann, K. A., J. L. Mobley-Tanaka, and J. M. Potter

2006 Style and Resistance in the Seventeenth Century Salinas Province. *American Antiquity* 71:621–647.

Spriggs, Matthew

1988 The Hawaiian Transformation of Ancestral Polynesian Society: Conceptualizing Chiefly States. In *The Emergence and Development of Social Hierarchy and Political Centralization*, edited by John Gledhill, Barbara Bender, and Mogens T. Larsen. Routledge, London: 57–72.

1989 God's Police and Damned Whores: Images of Archaeology in Hawaii. In *The Politics of the Past*, edited by Peter Gathercole and David Lowenthal, pp. 118–129. One World Archaeology 12. Unwin Hyman, London.

1991 Facing the Nation: Hawaiians and Archaeologists in an Era of Sovereignty. *The Contemporary Pacific* 3(2):379–392.

Spriggs, Matthew and Atholl Anderson

1993 Late Colonization of East Polynesia. *Antiquity* 67:200–217.

Spriggs, Matthew and Patrick V. Kirch

1992 *'Auwai, Kanawai*, and *Waiwai*: Irrigation in Kawailoa-Uka. In *Anahulu: The Anthropology of History in the Kingdom of Hawaii*, Chapter 4:118–164. 2 vols. University of Chicago Press, Chicago.

Starzecka, Dorota C.
  1975 *Hawaii: People and Culture*. British Museum Publications Limited, London.
Sterling, Elspeth P.
  1998 *Sites of Maui*. Bishop Museum Press, Honolulu.
Stevenson, Christopher M., Georgia Lee, and Frank J. Morin (editors)
  2001 *Pacific 2000: Proceedings of the Fifth International Conference on Easter Island and the Pacific*. Easter Island Foundation and Bearsville Press, Los Osos, California.
Stokes, John F. G.
  1906 *Hawaiian Nets and Netting*. Vol. 2. B. P. Bishop Museum Memoirs 1. Bishop Museum Press.
  1909a Notes on Hawaiian Petroglyphs I. *Occasional Papers of Bernice P. Bishop Museum* 4(4):257–295.
  1909b Walled Fish Traps of Pearl Harbor. *Occasional Papers of Bernice P. Bishop Museum* 4(3):199–212.
  1928 The Sacred Calabash. *Proceedings of the U.S. Naval Institute* 54(100): 138–139.
  1933 New Bases for Hawaiian Chronology. *Annual Report of the Hawaiian Historical Society* 41:23–65.
  1991 *Heiau of the Island of Hawai'i: A Historic Survey of Native Hawaiian Temple Sites*. Bishop Museum Bulletin in Anthropology 2. Edited and introduced by Tom Dye. Bishop Museum, Honolulu.
Storey, Alice A., Jose Miguel Ramirez, Daniel Quiroz, David V. Burney, David Addison, Richard Walter, Atholl J. Anderson, Terry L. Hunt, J. Stephen Athens, Leon Huynen, and Elizabeth Matisoo-Smith
  2007 Radiocarbon and DNA Evidence for a Pre-Columbian Introduction of Polynesian Chickens to Chile. *Proceedings of the National Academy of Sciences* 104:10335–10339.
Summers, Catherine C.
  1971 *Molokai: A Site Survey*. Pacific Anthropological Records 14. Anthropology Department, B. P. Bishop Museum, Honolulu.
  1989 *Hawaiian Cordage*. Pacific Anthropological Records 39. Anthropology Department, B. P. Bishop Museum, Honolulu.
  1999 *Material Culture: The J. S. Emerson Collection of Hawaiian Artifacts*. Bishop Museum Press, Honolulu.
Sweeney, Maria
  1992 Settlement Pattern Change in Hawai'i: Testing a Model for the Cultural Response to Population Collapse. *Asian Perspectives* 31:39–56.
Tainter, Joseph A.
  1973 The Social Correlates of Mortuary Patterning at Kaloko, North Kona, Hawaii. *Archaeology and Physical Anthropology in Oceania* 8:1–11.
  1991 The Kaloko Cemetery. In *An Ahupua'a Study: The 1971 Archaeological Work at Kaloko Ahupua'a, North Kona, Hawaii*. Western Archeological and Conserva-

tion Center Publications in Anthropology 58. National Park Service, U.S. Department of the Interior, Honolulu.

Tainter, Joseph A. and Ross H. Cordy
1977 An Archaeological Analysis of Social Ranking and Residence Groups in Prehistoric Hawaii. *World Archaeology* 9:95–112.

Takayama, Jun and Roger C. Green
1970 Excavations of Three Additional Field Shelters in Archaeological Zone 1. In *Makaha Valley Historical Project: Interim Report No. 2*, edited by Roger C. Green, Chapter 4:35–54. Pacific Anthropological Records 10. Anthropology Department, B. P. Bishop Museum, Honolulu.

Taylor, R. E.
1987 *Radiocarbon Dating: An Archaeological Perspective*. Academic Press, New York.

Thomas, Nicholas
2002 Colonizing Cloth: Interpreting the Material Culture of Nineteenth-Century Oceania. In *The Archaeology of Colonialism*, edited by Claire L. Lyons and John K. Papadopoulos, pp. 182–198. Getty Research Institute, Los Angeles, California.

Thrum, Thomas G.
1906–1907a Tales from the Temples. *Hawaiian Almanac and Annual*:49–69, 48–78.
1906–1907b Heiaus and Heiau Sites throughout the Hawaiian Islands. Island of Kauai. *Hawaiian Almanac and Annual*:36–48, 38–47.
1915 Completing Oʻahu's Heiau Search. *Hawaiian Almanac and Annual*:87–91.
1916 Maui's Heiaus and Heiau Sites Revised. *Hawaiian Almanac and Annual*:52–61.

Thurston, Lucy G.
1882 *Life and Times of Mrs. Lucy G. Thurston, Wife of Rev. Asa Thurston, Pioneer Missionary to the Sandwich Islands, Gathered from Letters and Journals of Extending Over a Period of More Than Fifty Years*. S. C. Andrews, Ann Arbor, Michigan.

Titcomb, Margaret
1972 *Native Use of Fish in Hawaii*. University Press of Hawaii, Honolulu.
1978 Native Use of Marine Invertebrates in Old Hawaii. *Pacific Science* 32:325–391.

Tomonari-Tuggle, Myra J.
2006 *Archaeological Data Recovery Investigations for the Northern Portion of Captain Cook Ranch*. International Archaeological Research Institute, Honolulu. Submitted to Captain Cook Ranch.

Townsend, W. H.
1969 Stone and Steel Tool Use in a New Guinea Society. *Ethnology* 8:199–205.

Tuggle, H. David
2010 Lady Mondegreen's Hopes and Dreams: Three Brief Essays on Inference in Hawaiian Archaeology. In *Research Designs for Hawaiian Archaeology*, edited by Thomas S. Dye, Chapter 3:157–184. Special Publications 3. Society for Hawaiian Archaeology, Honolulu.

Tuggle, H. David and P. Bion Griffin (editors)
1973 *Lapakahi, Hawaii: Archaeological Studies*. Asian and Pacific Archaeology Series 5. Social Science Research Institute, University of Hawaii, Honolulu.

Tuggle, H. David and Matthew Spriggs
2001 The Age of the Bellows Dune Site, O18, Oʻahu, Hawaiʻi, and the Antiquity of Hawaiian Colonization. *Asian Perspectives* 39(1–2):165–188.

Tuggle, H. David and Myra J. Tomonari-Tuggle
1980 Prehistoric Agriculture in Kohala, Hawaiʻi. *Journal of Field Archaeology* 7:287–312.

Turner, Christy and Jacqueline A. Turner
1999 *Man Corn: Cannibalism and Violence in the Prehistoric American Southwest*. University of Utah Press, Salt Lake City.

Upham, Steadman
1982 *Polities and Power: An Economic and Political History of the Western Pueblo*. Academic Press, New York.

Upton, Dell and John M. Vlatch
1986 *Common Places: Readings in American Vernacular Architecture*. University of Georgia Press, Athens.

Valeri, Valerio
1985a *Kingship and Sacrifice: Ritual and Society in Ancient Hawaii*. University of Chicago Press, Chicago.
1985b The Conqueror Becomes King: A Political Analysis of the Hawaiian Legend of ʻUmi. In *Transformations of Polynesian Culture*, edited by Antony Hooper and Judith Huntsman, pp. 79–103. Memoirs of the Polynesian Society 45. Polynesian Society, Auckland, New Zealand.
1990 Diarchy and History in Hawaii and Tonga. In *Culture and History in the Pacific*, edited by Jukka Siikala, pp. 45–79. Transactions of the Finnish Anthropological Society 27. The Finnish Anthropological Society, Helsinki.
1991 The Transformation of a Transformation: A Structural Essay on an Aspect of Hawaiian History (1809 to 1819). In *Clio in Oceania: Toward a Historical Anthropology*, edited by Aletta Biersack, pp. 101–164. Smithsonian Institution Press, Washington, DC.

Van Dyke, Jon M.
2008 *Who Owns the Crown Lands of Hawaiʻi?* University of Hawaii Press, Honolulu.

Van Gilder, Cindy
2001 Gender and Household Archaeology in Kahikinui, Maui. In *Pacific 2000: Proceedings of the Fifth International Conference on Easter Island and the Pacific*, edited by Christopher M. Stevenson, Georgia Lee, and Frank J. Morin. Easter Island Foundation and Bearsville Press, Los Osos, California.

Vitousek, Peter M., Thegn N. Ladefoged, Patrick V. Kirch, A. S. Hartshorn, Michael W. Graves, S. C. Hotchkiss, S. Tuljapurkar, and O. A. Chadwick
2004 Soils, Agriculture, and Society in Precontact Hawaiʻi. *Science* 304:1665–1669.

Webster, David
1998 Warfare and Status Rivalry: Lowland Maya and Polynesian Comparisons. In *Archaic States*, edited by Gary M. Feinman and Joyce Marcus, pp. 311–352. School of American Research, Santa Fe, New Mexico.

Weiner, Annette B. and Jane Schneider
1989 *Cloth and Human Experience*. Smithsonian Institution Press, Washington, DC.

Weisler, Marshall I.
1990 A Technological, Petrographic, and Geochemical Analysis of the Kapohaku Adze Quarry, Lanai, Hawaiian Islands. *New Zealand Journal of Archaeology* 12:29–50.
1993 The Importance of Fish Otoliths in Pacific Island Archaeofaunal Analysis. *New Zealand Journal of Archaeology* 15:131–159.
1998a Characterization of Archaeological Volcanic Glass from Oceania: The Utility of Three Techniques. In *Archaeological Obsidian Studies: Method and Theory*, edited by M. Steven Shackley, pp. 103–128. Plenum Press, New York.
1998b Hard Evidence for Prehistoric Interaction in Polynesia. *Current Anthropology* 39:521–532.
2011 A Quarried Landscape in the Hawaiian Islands. *World Archaeology* 43:298–317.

Weisler, Marshall I. and Patrick V. Kirch
1985 The Structure of Settlement Space in a Polynesian Chiefdom: Kawela, Molokai, Hawaiian Islands. *New Zealand Journal of Archaeology* 7:129–158.

Weisler, Marshall I. and Richard Walter
2002 Late Prehistoric Fishing Adaptations at Kawākiu Nui, West Molokaʻi. *Hawaiian Archaeology* 8:42–61.

Weisler, Marshall I., Kenneth D. Collerson, Yue-Xing Feng, Jian-Xin Zhao, and Ke-Fu Yu
2005 Thorium-230 Coral Chronology of a Late Prehistoric Hawaiian Chiefdom. *Journal of Archaeological Science* 33(2):273–282.

White, Tim D.
1992 *Prehistoric Cannibalism at Mancos 5MTUMR-2346*. Princeton University Press, Princeton, New Jersey.

Williams, Scott S.
1989 A Technological Analysis of the Debitage Assemblage from Koʻokoʻolau Rockshelter No. 1, Mauna Kea Adze Quarry, Hawaiʻi. MA thesis. Washington State University, Pullman.
2002 *Ecosystem Management Program, Cultural Resources Inventory Survey of Previously Unsurveyed Areas, Redleg Trail Vicinity, U.S. Army Pohakuloa Training Area, Island of Hawaiʻi, Hawaiʻi*. Ogden Environmental and Energy Services, Honolulu. Submitted to U.S. Army Engineer District.

2004   The Pohakuloa Chill Glass Quarry Complex, U.S. Army Pohakuloa Training Area, Hawaii Island. *Hawaiian Archaeology* 9:105–118.

Wilmshurst, Janet M., Atholl J. Anderson, Thomas F. G. Higham, and Trevor H. Worthy
2008   Dating the Late Prehistoric Dispersal of Polynesians to New Zealand Using the Commensal Pacific Rat. *Proceedings of the National Academy of Sciences* 105(22):7676–7680.

Wilmshurst, Janet M., Terry L. Hunt, Carl P. Lipo, and Atholl J. Anderson
2011   High-Precision Radiocarbon Dating Shows Recent and Rapid Initial Human Colonization of East Polynesia. *Proceedings of the National Academy of Sciences* 108(5):1815–1820.

Wittfogel, Karl
1957   *Oriental Despotism.* Yale University Press, New Haven, Connecticut.

Wobst, H. M.
1977   Stylistic Behavior and Information Exchange. In *For the Director: Research Essays in Honor of James B. Griffin,* edited by Charles Cleland, pp. 317–342. Anthropological Papers 61. Museum of Anthropology, University of Michigan, Ann Arbor.

Wolforth, Thomas R.
2005   Searching for Archaeological Manifestations of Hawaiian Battles on the Island of Hawaii. In *The Reñaca Papers, VI International Conference of Rapa Nui and the Pacific,* edited by Christopher M. Stevenson, J. M. Ramírez, F. J. Morin, and N. Barbacci, pp. 161–179. The Easter Island Foundation, Los Osos, California.

Wyban, Carol Araki
1992   *Tide and Current: Fishponds of Hawai'i.* University of Hawaii Press, Honolulu.

Yen, Douglas E., Patrick V. Kirch, Paul Rosendahl, and Thomas Riley
1972   Prehistoric Agriculture in the Upper Makaha Valley, Oahu. In *Makaha Valley Historical Project: Interim Report No. 4,* edited by Edmund J. Ladd, pp. 59–94. Pacific Anthropological Records 18. Anthropology Department, B. P. Bishop Museum, Honolulu.

Yoffee, Norman
2005   *Myths of the Archaic State: Evolution of the Earliest Cities, States, and Civilizations.* Cambridge University Press, Cambridge.

Young Leslie, H. and P. A. Addo
2007   Pacific Textiles, Pacific Cultures: Hybridity and Pragmatic Creativity. *Pacific Arts: The Journal of the Pacific Arts Association.*

Ziegler, Alan C.
2002   *Hawaiian Natural History, Ecology, and Evolution.* University of Hawai'i Press, Honolulu.

Index

barkcloth, 4, 38, 67, 68, 82, 89–90,
104–107, 111-112
Barrera Jr., William, 69
Bayman, James M., 9, 11, 69, 77–79, 99,
102, 105
Beaglehole, John C., 3, 37
Beckwith, Martha W., 4
Bell, Edward, 103
Bellows dune (O18 site), Oʻahu, 21–22, 31,
33
Bennett, Wendell C., 5
Bhabha, Homi K., 100, 112
Bishop Museum, vi, 4–7, 70–71, 106, 109,
119
Bishop, Sereno, 106
Bligh, William, 37
Bloxam, Andrew, 89–90
bowls, 4, 67, 69, 80, 90
Bowman, Sheridan, 22
breadfruit, 24, 37–38, 40, 122
Brigham, William T., 4, 67, 81, 102, 108
Brock, P., 105, 107
Brumfiel, Elizabeth M., 68, 77–78
Brunskill, R. W., 107
Buck, Caitlin E., 23, 24, 48, 51
Buck, Peter H., 4, 20, 67, 81, 89, 91, 108
burials
human, 5, 63, 90, 117–119
Burney, David A., 18, 23
Burtchard, Greg C., 49, 52
Byron, George Anson, 81, 103

Cachola-Abad, C. Kehaunani, 7, 120
calibration
Bayesian, 48, 58
Callaghan, Richard, 40
Calugay, Cyril, 73, 75
Cameron, Catherine, 107
Campbell, Archibald, 110
candlenut (kukui), 37–39, 65, 121
canoes, 2, 4, 13, 15–16, 21, 60, 63, 65,
67–69, 71, 84, 86, 90, 101–103, 105,
108, 121–122
capes
feather, 4, 67, 81
Carneiro, Robert L., 41
Carter, Laura A., 99

caves
shelter, 5, 60, 63–64, 75, 89–90, 119
ceramics, 6, 93–94
Chatan, R., 99
Chauvin, Michael E., 9
Cheever, Henry T, 102
chickens, 2, 37–38, 40, 61, 122
chiefdoms, 8, 27, 35, 83, 93, 100
chieftainship, 92
Chinen, Jon J., 117
Chiu, Min-yung, 62
Clarke, Andrew C., 38, 40
Cleghorn, Paul L., 6, 9, 69, 71, 75, 77, 79,
101
Clerke, Charles, 37
cloaks
feather, 4, 67, 81, 85, 104
Cobb, Charles R., 101
Cobb, John N., 55, 103
coconut, 2, 22, 37–38
Coiffier, Christian, 107
Collerson, Kenneth D., 9, 80
Collins, Sara L., 62, 64
colonialism, 11, 99, 101, 111–113, 115
commoners, 63, 78, 81–82, 89–90, 94–95,
100, 102–104, 107, 109, 111–112,
116–117
contact
Western, 2, 4, 8, 11, 27, 29, 37, 51,
67–71,77, 79–82, 84–85, 87, 89–92,
94–97, 99–106, 108, 111–113, 115
containers, 4, 38
Conte, Eric, 23
Cook, James, 1, 3, 4, 27, 37, 52, 67, 91, 99,
100, 104
Cordy, Ross H., 7–9, 26–27, 38, 90, 94–95,
98, 100
cores, salubrious, 29, 84
correlate method, 8, 27, 75, 83–84, 90,
91,93–94, 96–98
Costin, Cathy L., 75, 104
Crow Creek site, SD, 92
Cuddihy, Linda W., 18

Dalton, O. M, 67
dating
^{230}Th, 10

Wilmshurst, Janet M., 21, 23, 32
Wittfogel, Karl, 41
Wobst, H. M., 104
Wolforth, Thomas R., 91
Wood, Kenneth R., 18, 39
Wright, Rita P., 104
Wyban, Carol Araki, 55

Yen, Douglas E., 44, 47
Yoffee, Norman, 96–97
Young Leslie, H., 100

Ziegler, Alan C., 17–18, 38